New Remarks on the Passage to the Act

New Remarks on the Passage to the Act considers what happens when psychoanalysis and the social sciences are called on to help modern societies overwhelmed by unexplained violence.

Jean Allouch examines key events – the crimes of the Papin sisters, Lacan's case of Aimée and the murder of Hélène Rytmann by Louis Althusser – and unpacks the concept of the "passage to the act". The book assesses these classic cases, resorting to contemporaneous studies and literature, particularly discussing Marguerite Duras' novel *L'Amante Anglaise*. The book also considers modern acts of terrorism.

New Remarks on the Passage to the Act will be of great interest to clinicians, academics and scholars of psychoanalysis, Lacanian studies, sociology, cultural studies and philosophy, and to Lacanian analysts in practice and in training.

Jean Allouch (1939–2023) was an internationally renowned psychoanalyst and one of the founders and directors of the review *Littoral*, as well as of the École Lacanienne de Psychanalyse (Paris). He was one of the most prominent and prolific authors in the field of Lacanian psychoanalysis.

Oscar Zentner is a Lacanian psychoanalyst trained in Buenos Aires, Argentina, with María-Inés Rotmiler de Zentner, he introduced in 1977 Lacan's psychoanalytic tenets in Australia.

New Remarks on the Passage to the Act

Lacan and the Lacanians

Jean Allouch

Translated by Oscar Zentner

LONDON AND NEW YORK

Designed cover image: Jump of Thomas Diet, freeride skier, January 2004. Spot Alberg, Saint Anton, Austria. Courtesy of Dominique Daher.

First published in English 2025
by Routledge
4 Park Square, Milton Park, Abingdon, Oxon OX14 4RN

and by Routledge
605 Third Avenue, New York, NY 10158

Routledge is an imprint of the Taylor & Francis Group, an informa business

© 2025 Jean Allouch

The right of Jean Allouch to be identified as author of this work has been asserted in accordance with sections 77 and 78 of the Copyright, Designs and Patents Act 1988.

All rights reserved. No part of this book may be reprinted or reproduced or utilised in any form or by any electronic, mechanical, or other means, now known or hereafter invented, including photocopying and recording, or in any information storage or retrieval system, without permission in writing from the publishers.

Trademark notice: Product or corporate names may be trademarks or registered trademarks, and are used only for identification and explanation without intent to infringe.

First published in French as *Nouvelles remarques sur le passage à l'acte* by Epel Editions in 2019.

British Library Cataloguing-in-Publication Data
A catalogue record for this book is available from the British Library

ISBN: 978-1-032-82361-4 (hbk)
ISBN: 978-1-032-82360-7 (pbk)
ISBN: 978-1-003-50409-2 (ebk)

DOI: 10.4324/9781003504092

Typeset in Times New Roman
by KnowledgeWorks Global Ltd.

Contents

Foreword: Jean Allouch, in Memoriam   *vi*
Translator's Notes   *viii*
Presentation of "New Remarks on the Passage to
   the Act" by Jean Allouch   *x*
Provenance of Texts   *xxii*
Acknowledgements   *xxiii*

Introduction   1

I   Actuality of the Passage to the Act   11

II   To Think, to Act: Louis Althusser   27

III   Passage to the Act and the Epic Leap:
    Marguerite Duras   42

Conclusion: Enlightened Passage to the
   Act: Jacques Lacan   *70*
Index   *83*

Foreword

Jean Allouch, *in Memoriam*

Oscar Zentner

My completion of the translation of this pivotal work unhappily coincided with the death of its author, Jean Allouch, altering many givens, even though one knows that nothing can be taken for granted. It is unavoidable for me not to go back in time – to contextualise how I arrived at this page of this book.

I met Jean Allouch in Paris, in 1982, in the bitter and contested aftermath of Lacan's dissolution of *L'École freudienne de Paris*, and his death. It was a crowded and complicated gathering composed mainly, but not exclusively, of analysts and members of the dissolved school (who were themselves split into different sub-groups of "those in favour and those against" Lacan's dissolution. This gathering took place at Claude Dumezil's house, where discussions concerning different propositions were loud and heated. The disagreements aired in these discussions were not totally new, but they had been less apparent while Lacan was alive.

As chance would have it, I was on the same side as Jean, that is to say in favour of the dissolution. But now, more importantly, after the test of time I can also add that I was in agreement with his account of psychoanalysis. Though at the time we hardly exchanged more than a few words, since that occasion we managed to stay in contact, despite long gaps imposed by the distance across the ocean. His friendly generosity was manifested through the sending of his books as they were published. And it was then that I took up the custom of reading his works twice, first in French and later in Spanish. In parallel and whenever possible I also attended his seminars. During these years a trusting relationship was formed, as demonstrated by his readiness to accept my idea to translate his book into English.

In our long-distance correspondence, it became customary that each one wrote to the other in his own mother tongue, he used his French and I used my Spanish, yet whenever we were face-to-face, we only spoke Spanish. His Spanish was impeccable, and I think he knew this and was proud of it. When relevant, I commented to him on my reading and writing projects. I recall one such exchange that gives an idea of Jean's straightforward manner; I had sent him something I'd written and after a time I got his answer:

Cher Óscar, et où sont les cent pages manquantes ...?[1]

His irony was a proof of his friendship because it contained a discreet prompt, with effects as long lasting as they were invaluable. But above and beyond anything else, I would like to emphasise what in my opinion was fundamental to his psychoanalytic tenets, and very likely – as I told him after reading this book – what Allouch obtained from his analysis and silence with Lacan, something – again in my opinion – similar to his "*Je m'en fiche de Lacan*".[2] This "*I don't care*" allowed him not only to read, study and question his ex-analyst without any misplaced loyalty, but also to continue many of the ideas left obscured, truncated or unresolved in many of Lacan's propositions. In other words, to become the analyst he was. You can read his own words on the matter:

> *Where my "I don't care about Lacan" will have worked.*
>
> I went to Lacan exactly like someone for whom it was possible not to care about. You don't come across someone of this ilk on every street corner. Because it is one thing not to care about someone, and another not to care together with that someone or at least not without him. I have just told you my definition of a psychoanalyst.

Allouch was undoubtedly one of the most important analysts who came out from Lacan's couch (I refrain, with good reason, from using the adjective "Lacanian"). He had a unique and thorough knowledge of Lacan's seminars and references. He was cultured and well-versed in literature and philosophy and had the rare ability to treat difficult psychoanalytic matters with extreme clarity and rigour. The book that you are about to read is an excellent proof of this and absolves me from going further. His death is a great loss for psychoanalysis – and you will see why.

Jean Allouch's unexpected death is what makes my Foreword stop here, for I considered its only viable continuation would be *my silence* and Allouch's own words – words that he stated when invited by Encore Paris in 2019 to expound the main propositions contained in his (at that time) recent work. It is this same presentation that I choose as the best way for the English reader first encounter his work.

O.Z., Melbourne, March 2024

Notes

1 Dear Oscar, and where are the missing one hundred pages?
2 Allouch, Jean, Je m'en fiche de Lacan, 9 Saloon international de psychiatrie, Sorbonne, 13 November 2001.

Translator's Notes

I should begin by telling the reader that Allouch was a dear friend of mine as well as an exemplary analyst. He was, in brief, someone from whom to learn meant being shaken from our certitudes, that is to say, from our prejudices; and, in consequence, I approached this translation as an analyst and reader of his writings.

The present situation of psychoanalysis has been in the main reduced to a commonplace repetition of ideas; formulaic platitudes that, under the umbrella of Freud and Lacan, give place to a despairing discourse of Babylonian proportions.

The present book addresses and maps many of the quicksands in which the psychoanalyst and psychoanalysis are immersed. In a rigorous and inexorable way, it uncovers theoretical and clinical misconceptions. It was written with the uncommon quality of having its subject matter treated with clear and rigorous style. It is precisely this latter that constituted my concern from beginning to the end; how to convey Jean Allouch's style, including his neologisms to English equivalents, while retaining their meaning. To this end I entrusted myself less to the unavoidable famous or rather infamous *traduttore traditore*, and in this case more specifically to our "*faux amis*".

I approached the task with an altogether different perspective, one that was directly linked to my participation in a seminar given by Allouch in 2009 in Buenos Aires where, at the moment of questions and answers, I commented something along the lines of "better to be mistaken by your own counsel than by someone else's", illustrating the point with the Spanish (Creole) proverb "*Nada mejor que perderse para hacerse baqueano*" (the conference moved easily between French and Spanish), to which, as I remember, Allouch retorted by saying that he liked it and that he would adopt it. And, as it happens, I considered the proverb the best suited for this translation as well as for approaching psychoanalysis.

Last but not least, this book varies from the French version in the following aspects. I am responsible for the variations, as they were my sole choice:

- The English version has a subtitle, *Lacan and the Lacanians* of the book.
- The English version has incorporated the presentation to the conference that Allouch was invited to give on 14 December 2018 at Encore, Paris,

on his (at that time) forthcoming book, *New Remarks on the Passage to the Act*. Although never proposed by Allouch for his book, again, it has been my choice to include it as a statement, because who better than Allouch himself to introduce the theme with his own words when presenting the main tenets of the book he was close to finishing at the time.

Jean Allouch's own words and explanation will give the reader a valuable indication of the way he would add a final touch of many of his books by giving seminars on a particular subject, testing them by proposing novel ways, answering questions from the audience and thus reworking or fine-tuning many of his propositions, which in the main, if proven correct, usually finished in an article or a book.

Oscar Zentner
19 December 2024
Melbourne, Australia

Presentation of "New Remarks on the Passage to the Act" by Jean Allouch[1]

First and foremost, thank you for your kind invitation to address a question that I am very keen to share with you. A question that I could call mine "since forever", at least since my childhood or even before I was born, to know that of madness. I situate it in this way – and perhaps you will agree because madness also affects you, *professionally*, through the intermediary of psychoanalysis or psychiatric practice. As you know, first Freud, then Michel Foucault and Jacques Lacan, moved away from the medical bias, notably Foucault who cited Pascal in his *Madness and Civilization: A History of Insanity in the Age of Reason*: "Men are so necessarily mad, that not to be mad would amount to another kind of madness."

Whoever has read this decisive work would have learned that, with "this other kind of madness", Foucault designated the nascent psychiatry, in which I underline with Pinel and much later with Henry Ey[2] that the definition of alienism implies the word freedom. One can write this as: S1 $\longrightarrow$ S2. Lacan also rejected the distinction "mad"/"not mad", there is nothing about two sides for him, with a wall in between on one side this confinement of *holding of* few people justified as *containing the mentally ill, the others* discriminating the sane; there is no *us* and *them* whatsoever. Notably, when the fashion was to use "psychopath", as today, "narcissistic perverse", "autistic" and earlier "neurasthenic" – and so many more imaginary entities constructed, Lacan said, relying on the forging of the term "psychopath", "How have we not realised that everyone suffers from having a soul?" (I quote by heart). Here we have "soul" replacing "psyche", as it was with Kraepelin, who used *Seelenstörungen*, "disorders of the soul", and not "psychoses". Lacan made the point to emphasise that if a psychotic is someone inhabited by "imposed words", it is the same for everyone: "How we do not feel, that the words on which we depend are in a way not imposed on us?". He said, about a paraphrenic presenting a cosmological delusion, "Well, yes he is someone like me, a dogmatic". [*Translator's note*: Lacan said elsewhere something alike to psychosis being an attempt at rigour.] Was this a self-diagnosis?

Other Lacanian references could easily lead to the opposite conclusion; Lacan has continued to maintain a ternary nosography: neuroses, perversion, psychosis.[3] Yet, the use of this psychiatric- psychoanalytic register was a kind of mistake that, for me, signalled his uneasiness with it. One remembers the unfortunate presentation of a patient, a transsexual, during which Lacan made the audience laugh at the patient's expense. This was something that immediately horrified me, particularly since I believed the case to be unique. During this presentation the patient was made fun of in his presence and at his expense (the "second person" of the joke according to Freud). Lacan was also wrong regarding Antonin Artaud, when he stated, as if his knowledge allowed him to foresee the future: "This fellow will never write again" – something that turned out to be completely false. Like others, Lacan also changed his diagnosis: Marguerite Anzieu was first presented as having a "self-punishing paranoia", but much later on, this was considered to be an erotomania – which also was not true. There is nothing exceptional in this. We can recall the so-called "Wolf man": how many diagnoses has he been given (by those who received him and by the many who have commented on his case)? Freud sees him as neurotic, Ruth Mack Brunswick sees him, in fact, as paranoid, Lacan sees him as psychotic (although he abandons this label), Serge Leclaire speaks of him as having "a psychotic episode".

In short, these fluctuations and others like them lead us to affirm that this way of treating patients as different from oneself made Lacan uncomfortable. I have deduced that such divisions can be abandoned without any loss – indeed, quite the contrary at least in the Freudian field as well as in psychopathology. In dismissing psychopathology, I am ignoring that it could have opposed nosography and be proposed as another and new paradigm for psychiatry (Lantéri-Laura). Certainly, Freud used the term "psychopathology" as the title of a work [*The psychopathology of everyday life*] whose innovative scope cannot be underestimated. [*Translator's note*: Allouch refers to it since in this work, there is not any division between them(the mentally ill) and us (the mentally sane).] We have noticed, however, that there is an abyss between the way Freud defines this term applying to people who are not recognised as mentally ill (in their everyday life) and the definition of Marie-Claude Lambotte in *Le Discours mélancolique: de la phénoménologie à la métapsychologie*. Both works apart from the ambiguity regarding the term "psychopathology" do not have anything in common.

Something we should not forget, in the background, as noted by Georges Lantéri-Laura,[4] is that three paradigms succeeded one another in the history of psychiatry, not without sometimes overlapping one another:[5] the *mental alienation* paradigm of Pinel to Falret;[6] the paradigm of *mental illnesses*, when Falret (mid-19th century) put forward their plurality, rejecting the Pinelian unity of mental alienation; the paradigm of *psychopathological structures*, launched in Geneva in 1926 during the 30th session of the Congrès des Médecins Aliénistes, when Bleuler presented his concept of the group of schizophrenias – a third paradigm of which, according to Lantéri-Laura, Henri Ey's death in 1977 signalled the beginning of the end. Twenty years ago, Lantéri-Laura added: "Except for abused of knowledge, we do not know anything of what could have been the paradigm of psychiatry since the last quarter of our XX century. After all, we would happily say: too bad for us."[7]

The worldwide adoption of the North American statistical paradigm proves these words of De Gaulle: "Power is not taken, it is collected." So here we are ... psychiatrists, inhabitants of a desert where this new statistical paradigm has easily been established; and now, the neurosciences are searching the brain for an equivalent of what Gall and phrenology were searching for: the bump of crime, or of madness.[8] And psychoanalysis, with its step aside from psychiatry? If it recuses the ultimate statistical paradigm, it is less in the clear with the three preceding paradigms, participating more or less in each of them. Thus, psychoanalysis proves to be Pinelian each time that it tries to produce a unitary version of madness, as this is where its concept of a "psychic apparatus" (Freud) or a "structure of the subject" is invited. There are neither two psychic apparatuses in Freud, nor two structures of the subject in Lacan. Psychoanalysis is also Falretienne when it is based on the clinical ternary of neurosis/psychosis/perversion: it participates in the third paradigm when it unfolds a psychopathologising discourse.

Viewed after the publication of these *Nouvelles remarques sur le passage à l'acte*, I think I can say that this work has opened a zone (a cherished term by the Zadists to Mayette Viltard to Patricia Janody) where a new version of the passage to the act could be inscribed. The work was written in close theoretical dependence on Lacan and clinical dependence on Fethi Benslama's recent discovery of the "epic leap".

Clearing an area that provides a place for a new problematisation of the passage to the act requires a few thrusts – a bit like making your way through a packed crowd. It was necessary to push aside a certain number of comments made about the passage to the act, from three different points of view.

I

First of all the Lacanians, and even former comrades. Those I criticised in the book have completely eliminated the passage to the act, reabsorbing it in a version of the act that they claim to have received from Lacan. They entitled their work "To pass to the act", a very clear allusion to the passage to the act. However, seemingly nothing in this formula includes the passage to the act, because whoever passes to the act, does not intend like them to "pass to the act". Curiously while Lacan gave battle to the psychoanalysts of the International Psychoanalytic Association (IPA, an acronym that Laurie Laufer read as "Industrie Psychanalytique Actuelle") they concur in the end with the same thing as a psychoanalyst from the [IPA], whose work I also dispute. They do this by drowning the passage to the act in a soggy concept of the act, while Marie-Claude Lambotte, the analyst from the IPA, without realising it, shows that the set of ethical rules and practices that they give themselves in their group have no other purpose than to avoid at all cost the passage to the act, especially that of the psychoanalyst. To avoid, in French (*éviter*) is close to (*inviter*), if it is true that a deviation from "Never again" (sex) often turns into "more than ever" (Lacan). The aforementioned Lacanians avoid passing to the act by making it disappear from their field. One will search in vain in their work for an analysis of these acting outs which nevertheless indeed occupied Lacan: those of the Papin sisters, of Marguerite Anzieu, of the "Young homosexual woman". It remains to be assessed whether these were indeed, as he said, acting outs. No mention either, in their work, of the passage to the act, of Iris Cabezudo or of the teacher Wagner – of which, we should moreover wonder here too, if they were instead questions of epic leaps. On the other hand, the work of Carlos Busqued, *The four crimes of Ricardo Melogno*, currently published by Epel, clearly reports strangely similar passages to the act. A novelist talks to the criminal and having no other intention than to speak with him with a view to publication, gets something much different from what a therapist would have him say.

With this book, I proposed to establish another and different relation in regard to the passage to the act, less fearful and timid, not even paradoxical, encouraging to no longer consider it as the thing to be avoided above all else, the worst that there is. Because there is a fear of the passage to the act,[9] which notably makes us forget that if "*madness is a disease of freedom*" (Henry Ey) *it is by addressing the madman, not as an insane person but as a free being, that one can help him realise that he is exercising his freedom even within his madness*. This fear impedes us to see a passage to the act in minor gestures (for example, breaking a stack of plates, burning newspapers [Claire Lannes] or leaving the room by slamming the door), because the first manifestation that we think of at the mere mention of the syntagm "passage to the act" is either death or suicide.

This haunting is one of the signs of a fearful relationship with death. Phillipe Ariès was the first to establish that after the 1914–1918 "hecatomb", the West turned away from death impeding any problematisation and thus it made it savage or, as I call it, "dry";[10] as such (as if forbidden to talk about it), we lose the way of "taming it", of knowing how to deal with it, as far as this is possible if [death] is, as Lacan dixit "the absolute master", and this dryness is found in the widespread avoidance of the passage to the act.

If it is true that haunting never is good counsel, one will agree that this avoidance of death (this refusal of the death drive, a refusal that Lacan wanted to put to an end by linking it to the symbolic) poses a problem for the practitioner, without him even knowing it. This hardens his position; it does not give him freedom to reign; it does not leave him free to intervene. He will only find this freedom by being partially aware of what has been called for ages (the Bible, ancient India) "the between two deaths",[11] which is, forgive me, the very place where madness take place. Suicide or murder remain inaccessible if one shares the common belief, according to which, for everyone, life is the most precious thing there is. Suicides are so numerous today in the West, it is said that this offers proof that this is not the case.

II

It was also necessary to discard the common idea of the passage to the act as conveyed by the media, opening their columns to experts, sociologists, psychiatrists and psychoanalysts. A jihadist murder is not a passage to the act, as they keep saying and writing. Why? Because it is part of a story that, precisely, makes the between deaths a place beyond physical death. In this it differs from the crime of the Papin sisters, which remains forever without explanation, to the point that, very early on, literature, cinema and theatre took over from the lively psychiatric discussions to which this violent passage to the act immediately gave rise without anyone ever having the last word. The support taken, or not, on a story discriminates the passage to the act and the epic leap, which recognises and sometimes announces what motivates it, and is carried out with knowledge of the cause, even if it is not with *whole knowledge* of the cause.

III

It was also necessary to set aside certain comments from Lacan that gave the impression that something, sometimes a word, a phrase, would manifest itself in the act in lieu of being uttered or said. Exemplary in this regard was for him the so-called[12] "passage to the act" of Freud's patient "the young homosexual woman", known as Margarethe Csonka. According to the first presentation he made of it, her passage to the act would have represented childbirth, playing in the two meanings of *niederkommen* ("to let fall" and "to give birth"), therefore this is what she would have done by throwing herself over the parapet of a bridge spanning a railway line; giving birth would be what the passage to the act would be, what the passage to the act would have meant. This supposed word (by Lacan relying on Freud) would have been *passed* to the act or better *in* the act: "I too, like my mother who is now pregnant, want to give birth to my father's child." Such so-called interpretations make me laugh. Why wouldn't she simply say these words, she so free, to the point of loving, at fourteen, to the great dismay of her family, a prostitute (vaguely connected to the nobility)?[13] We do not know! However, we usually approach the passage to the act with such a "psychoanalytic" theory, which assumes that the passage to the act carries a saying that cannot be expressed in words. This theory is, upon examination, nothing other than a prejudice reinforced by a Lacan of 1950s. What is more, this prejudice opened the door wide to a hope put into speech, which it can be considered as truly despairing – if it remains true that hope is the royal road open to suicide.[14]

The specification we did above permits that a new conceptualisation of the passage to the act could take place, taking in an experience both trivial and common. Thomas Diet, the freestyle skier featured on the cover of this book who jumped a dizzying rock face, put it in one phrase, his motto: "To think is to capitulate." This is true in other sports as well ... if I think, when returning a ball on a tennis court, "Where am I going to return it, in the forehand or the backhand of my opponent?", every time it will end up in the net. The same goes for whatever decision we are about to implement.

At the time when a group of us went to lie on Lacan's couch,[15] a friend told us he spent his sessions wondering what name he was going to choose for his daughter who was about to be born. Every time he thought of a name, he discovered in the session all the horrors he was about to impose on her, so he it gave up. I ignore how his problem could be solved. It could be that, thanks to the analysis, this girl never received a first name Thinking, analysing in *his own way,* that is to say insofar as he is thinking, will end in his own inhibition.

In Latin America, Argentinians are the object of witticisms, a little like Belgians in France, but for the opposite reasons: too much intelligence, the chatter of nerves. This is how they are seen by their Latino[16] friends. The wife of a friend living in Mexico told me this one. When a guy kisses a woman in Argentina, she told me amusedly, the woman, interrupting him with a wave of her hand, pushes him away saying: "Wait, I have to think about that." A Mexican woman, this same Mexican friend told me, reacting differently would say in modern language: "Cool, superb, keep going! It is good!" ... *Thinking inhibits the act*: one only has to point out to an obsessional symptom to have no doubt about it.[17] Lacan sealed this in a formula that took apart the Cartesian cogito and that, in its own way, says the same thing as the motto of my freestyle champion friend: "Where I think, I am not, where I am, I don't think." The analyst does not invite the analysand to say what he thinks but what comes to mind ... One will agree, it is very different. On the one hand, there is a master (a certain rigidity one might say), on the other hand, a letting go. When someone begins a sentence with "I think ...", you can be sure that he is somewhere other than what he is telling you. Would you recognise a declaration of love if someone says to you "I think that I love you"? No, you will leave him or her to his or her thoughts. "Love does not think, an effect of narcissism", noted Lacan.[18]

On this basis, I revisited the question of the passage to the act in the only way that I considered consistent with the analytical method, namely the careful, extensive and detailed study of cases, and not the misleading clinical vignettes. Lacan praised Freud for having published some cases in such a way that, based on the material Freud had reported, one can produce another and different interpretation from the Freudian one. I welcome this criterion as decisive. The case, like the dream, presents such a dense network of encrypted data that it forces its analysis not to get lost in untimely considerations. Commenting on a dream is not interpreting it – even if the person commenting on it is, whether he likes it or not, associating.

A chapter of this work is thus devoted to the murder of his wife by Louis Althusser who, at the time and afterwards, made a certain noise in the

Landerneau. Another chapter concerns the heroine of *L'Amante anglaise* (Marguerite Duras' novel). Claire Lannes had killed and cut into pieces the body of the niece of the man with whom she lives without loving him. It is, specially, the analysis of this last gesture, so violent, that appears as both a combination of passage to the act and the epic leap, which revealed itself to be a way of mourning. "The work of mourning" one could say, following Freud. Nonetheless, no: mourning above and beyond is not work, the same goes for love, there is no "work of love": Alain Badiou left this well-made expression regarding a prolonged and devitalised romantic relationship, when the two partners begin to get bored (weak word) with each other. Mourning and love are related to act, also separate, for which Lacan invented the concept of "*sé-partition*", that almost everyone does not care about.

Nowadays, mourning is Freudianly thought in the same ill-adjusted coordinates as is the passage to the act.[19] In madness too, mourning attempts to take place, just as in analyses. From the age of 14 to 18 years of age, every person in mourning has invented a unique way of grieving. A violent epic leap, such as that of Claire Lannes, can thus be received as a valid mode of mourning – its own. However, it is important to differentiate it from the passage to the act and this is what this work brings to light through these two murders.

In any case, it seems appropriate to me, here, with all of you who have read *L'acte psychanalitique*, to underscore a trait that, in my *New remarks on the passage to the act*, is a point addressed specially to the analyst taken to the point where his practice is most effective. It is about a concept that could be received as teratological, as it remains true that it is difficult to conceive what Lacan intended by speaking of "enlightened passage to the act" or even "informed". This curious passage to the act would mean for the analyst not thinking, because "it is by not thinking that he operates".[20] Precisely for this I can bear witness: during my years of analysis with him, not even once did Lacan share with me a thought that he had about me.

And it was so much better for me ... so much better for me, but also ... for him. *I analysed myself with him,*[21] this "*myself*" that the Spanish language carries with: "*Yo me analizo con*" and not, as in French or English, "*I was or I am in analysis with*". Such *myself* is sometimes what a child will use to an adult who is preparing to help him on a task he has given himself (for example, getting on a bicycle for the very first time). "No, by *myself*!" replies the child, dismissing the adult with a gesture, which the latter accepts if he realises to what extent this decision of the child is serious, even subjectively vital. Far from contravening love, leaving the other, this other loved, to be alone (on certain occasions) can be considered a gesture of love.[22]

According to the thread the "enlightened passage to the act", Lacan was led to define analysis as a "practice that by chance found itself opening up a complete different mode of action between humans".[23] With this definition we are a thousand miles away from thought. What would become of the entity known as "schizophrenia" if we gave up seeing it, with Bleuler, as a "thought disorder"? The example he gives of such a "disorder" is, to say the least, farcical. He asks a patient he recognises as schizophrenic, "Where is Egypt?" and receives as an answer, "Between Assyria and the State of Congo." He comments:

> Already the fact of associating in one's thoughts one of the oldest states in the world with one of the most modern is only possible when the notion of time which in normal man never fails to play its role in the unconscious fails in the patient (but could there be notions [including time] in the unconscious?). But to bring closer to the notion (again?) of Egypt is more bizarre from a geographical point of view. The most relevant idea such as "North Africa" does not arise in the patient, but on the other hand that of a country belonging to another continent and whose border doesn't touch Egypt, and then he associates another country which is only indirectly related to Egypt through Sudan. And yet the patient's response proved that he knew the geographical location of Egypt well.[24]

We are very happy to learn here that Eugen Bleuler knows his geography of Africa well. But Bleuler also remarks that the patient has a notion of time and space considered unhealthy, and, just after having collected this "faulty" response, Bleuler sees a "disorder of associations", a "loosening of associations" (therefore associations of ideas), a relaxation that is supposed to make thought abnormal, judged in terms of the psychiatrist. "Association" does not have the same signification as with Freud, for whom it does not matter what is associated with what, where everything is fine, where there is no good answer to be expected, as it is, as we have just seen, with Bleuler.[25] You can see here, what was the normative and unfriendly position towards the patient, of someone who for the very first time reported autism.

Is the notion, even the concept, of father, mother, child, or anything we can think of really in the unconscious? One is gently led to admitting this when considering with Freud that there are "unconscious thoughts".

Ensuring his/her thoughts remain silent, not being encumbered by them, this would be a question for the analyst. It would become his operational ascesis, that is to say, producing a certain effect on the analysand. We have a counterexample. A work by Serge Leclaire (may he rest in peace) had at the time, a certain editorial success, notably because it was published in a collection directed by Lacan and for the reason that it opened with Leclaire writing what an analyst (himself) thought while listening to someone.[26] Furthermore, the literary quality of this page leaves no room for doubt. At the opening of his *Psychoanalyzing: On the order of the Unconscious and Practice of the Letter*,[27] Leclaire unveiled and gave account of a secret – like a magician, who confuses his audience by announcing that he is going to reveal the secret of his trick in order to better prepare himself for the next round and, already, to complete this next round. Leclaire:

> Profiting from the patient's silence that reigns for a moment, before the patient comments on his fantasy, let us sit on the armchair in the secret of the psychoanalyst thoughts. He recognises there, immediately, without being able to defend himself from a slight discomfort given by a sentiment of familiarity [author's emphasis] a typical obsessive fantasm, this only confirms him, once again his diagnostic point of view of the patient, and our [sic] psychoanalyst lets himself thinking about the variants of this fantasy.

In these thoughts, where a practising ("Lacanian") psychoanalyst, retrieves his usual marks within his "patient words", we then expect Lacan to appear ... and here we have soon summoned, by our thinking psychoanalyst, the paraphernalia of "the Lacanian psychoanalytic knowledge", "the problem of identification", "Jacques Lacan princeps work, *The Mirror Stage* as formative of the I". Well here, among other things, is what Lacan wanted to avert with his invitation aimed at the analyst not to think and thus to operate. But how can we make him stop thinking? The analyst is silent in different fashions. Leclaire's thoughts seem to him to shed light on his patient's words. In what way does he abandon his place and his function as analyst? What is at stake here is not the accuracy, the pertinence, of what the analyst may have said, but more radically that those cumbersome thoughts do not become silent, leaving place to a certain silence that is not a withdrawal, but in which the silent presence of the analyst evokes the incompleteness of the Other.[28]

Wittgenstein knew how to maintain such a silence when referring to ethics, saying that he found himself "in front of the door to the solution, without seeing sufficiently clear[ly] how to open it". One of Pessoa's heteronyms shares this Wittgensteinian attitude, "he observes that to be totally clear and moral, one ought to be a bit stupid". "To be absolutely intellectual, one has to be a little immoral."[29] This silence of the analyst that I am trying to approach with you may appear to be a little immoral, as someone who abstains from highly prized caring, moreover, he un-cares (*décharite*).[30] Standing in front of a door without possessing the possibility of opening it, even when one wishes to pass to the other side, is not so easy, especially since the analysand, too, wishes to pass through this door, which momentarily halts his analysis while expecting his/her analyst to offer the means. A Wittgenstein, sometimes a Lacan, knew how not to escape this unappealing ordeal of remaining silent, to stay put in front of the door, although multiple evasions are possible, as evidenced by the uneasiness of Leclaire in revealing his secret. It does not take much to advance knowledge, even when one suspects he does not really have it, anyway it will give to those who utter it and to those who hear it the impression, the illusion of a breakthrough.

This very singular silence of the analyst intervenes with the analysand as what it is likely to do is to direct him towards the non-existence of the Other, this place where one does not find the expected solution, but another solution, at first rather disappointing when not traumatic (Lacan). This is how, in my opinion, the accesses of the analyst (the analyst without "psy")[31] operates, because the "psy" thinks too much to the point of being verbose. In *The Tempest*, Shakespeare says something without knowing, of course, that one day it would concern analysis, the effect this silence of the analyst produces in the analysand: *The man who speaks renounces his magic*. This being silent (that with Lacan, I say, is the silence of the analyst) leaves room for the realisation of this renunciation, which is due to the sole fact of speaking.

What kind of renunciation is this? Conjecture: It is the destitution of the persistent presence in mind and flesh of the sex envisaged as relation operating in the speech of the analysand as long as the analyst abstain for parasitised it with his own thoughts.

Thank you once more for your invitation to talk all this with you. I make mine the way Foucault addressed one of his audiences:

> *I think we are here mainly to discuss: this is to say that I should not talk at all. But, in any case, I suppose that, in order for you to be able to exercise your right to questions, which will be a right to examine and a right to criticise, I must expose myself to your blows, and consequently, I will present some remarks, a little disorderly, from which, it is my intention, you will have the opportunity to express yourselves.*

This remark was made in Tunis on 4 February 1967. It has just been published in a work whose importance for analysis cannot be ignored: *Folie, langage, littérature*, Paris, Vrin, 2019 (p. 170).

Notes

1 Jean Allouch, *Exposé sur Nouvelles remarques sur le passage à l'acte* (14 December 2019, p. 3). I very much thank Silvia Halac who, at my request sent me a copy of Jean Allouch's presentation. Encore, Paris, 2019.

2 I too made a case for it, as a statement in the position of an axiom (*La Scène lacanienne et son cercle magique*, Paris, Epel, 2017).

3 See my critique in "Perturbation in pernepsy", *Lacan love, Melbourne seminars and other works* edited by and Foreword by María-Inés Rotmiler de Zentner and Oscar Zentner (Lituraterre, Melbourne, 2007).

4 Georges Lantéri-Laura, *Essai sur les paradigmes de la psychiatrie moderne* (Paris, Éditions du Temps, 1998, p. 53). I owe the remainder of this reference to Guy Casadamont who mentions it in a work in preparation on Violette Nozière.

5 Thus Thierry Hausten and Jérémie Sinzelle write, in their valuable presentation "Emil Kraepelin": "In the middle of the XXth century, the Kraepelinian model of 'categorical' clinical entity is called into question. A unitary approach to mental disorders then tends to impose itself, together with the criticism of mental

institutions and the concept of illness in psychiatry. Thus promoting a rehabilitation of the 'medical' model emerges in the United States under the banner of Kraepelin, contemporary with the expansion of biological psychiatry." (I owe to Patrick Landman for the access to this article.)
6 "What are we doing [...] by supporting the doctrine of monomania?" Falret questions, and replies: "We are making impossible any strict line of demarcation between passion and madness." (Quoted by Marc Renneville, *Crime et folie. Deux siècles d'enquêtes médicales et judiciaires*, Paris, Fayard, 2003). Morel also rejects the doctrine of monomania, a "factitious entity". This cleared the way for his doctrine of degeneration, which a certain Sigmund Freud was to reject.
7 Georges Lantéri-Laura, *Essai sur les paradigmes de la psychiatrie moderne* (Paris, Éditions du Temps, 1998, p. 22).
8 Marc Renneville, *Crime and madness: Two centuries of medical and judicial investigations* (Paris, Fayard, 2003). Very rich in data, this work covers the history of psychiatry by considering it in its relationship to the legal system.
9 In this regard, we can watch the debate proposed by Patrick Landman: "Are psychotropic drugs the remedy for psychological suffering?" https://youtu.be/o6SUa6ubegI. Jean Allouch, *Exposé sur Nouvelles remarques sur le passage à l'acte* (14 December 2019, p. 5).
10 *Érotique du deuil au temps de la mort sèche* (Paris, Epel, 1997). La crémation sèche les corps.
11 See Jean Allouch, "Folie, première et seconde mort", *L'Évolution psychiatrique*, Vol. 81, no. 1, January-March 2016.
12 Jean Allouch, "Ledit" car j'ai montré qu'il ne s'agissait pas d'un passage à l'acte, *Ombre de ton chien. Discours psychanalytique, discours lesbien* (Paris, Epel, 2004).
13 Ines Rieder, Diana Voigt, *Homosexuelle chez Freud, lesbienne dans le siècle* (Paris, Epel, 2003).
14 Dominique Simonet regularly attends what happens in the courts and reports on it in *Le Canard enchaîné*, thus following in André Gide's footsteps. On 27 November 2019, his article chose as its title a statement by a certain Adrien, aged 29, tried at the Reims Assizes for having killed a certain Gaëtan, the same age: two shots from a shotgun through a glass door. We are waiting for motives, explanations. "I shot the door because I shot the door." His little brother had called him for help. "And for that you are capable of going as far as homicide?", he is asked. I am referring to this case only for his answer (to think about): "No, it is the unfolding [my emphasis] that brought me here."
15 Clarification: there were not five or six of us lying on Lacan's couch at the same time. We were returning from a distant suburban CMPP (Centre medico-psychopedagogique) crammed into the same car and we presented ourselves at the same time at the door of his consultation room.
16 This is demonstrated by a very well-known joke: "How does an Argentinian commit suicide?" Answer: "He climbs over his self and throws himself down."
17 Typical example (told by Freud). A motorist avoids a stone on a road. He soon stops, thinking that he should remove it from this place, from this route, because it could cause an accident. He clears the road, returns to his car and then thinks that his action is likely to cause an accident, because a motorist in a hurry would no longer be forced by the stone to moderate his excessive speed. He gets out of his car a second time and puts this stone back on the road. And so we ...
18 Jacques Lacan, *La Logique du fantasme*, 25 January 1967. Jean Allouch, *Exposé sur Nouvelles remarques sur le passage à l'acte* (14 December 2019, p. 8).
19 I explained this in *Érotique du deuil au temps de la mort sèche* (Paris, Epel, 1997). Jean Allouch, *Exposé sur Nouvelles remarques sur le passage à l'acte* (14 December 2019, p. 9).

20 Jacques Lacan, "Summary of the seminar The Psychoanalytic Act", where this statement was written, 1967–1968.
21 Jean-Luc Godard filmed a sequence where, in a café, a couple are talking. The young woman puts her partner on notice: "I'm not counting on you," she tells him, "I'm counting on you."
22 I explained it in Jean Allouch, *L'Amour Lacan* (Paris, Epel, 2009).
23 This quote is developed with more details on page 125 of these New Remarks on Acting Out.
24 Eugen Bleuler, "Schizophrenia", psychiatric report during the 30th session of the Congress of Alienists and Neurologists of France and French-speaking countries, 2–7 August 1926 (Paris, Masson, 1926).
25 Was "Assyria" such an unwelcome association? If "Egypt" evokes pyramids, pharaohs and other old things, associating it with "Assyria" is not inappropriate.
26 This procedure of Leclaire was used as a model in a recent work by Annie Frank, *Entrelacs* (Paris, Éditions des Crépuscules, 2019). The author presents a story of cures on the left-hand page and, on the right-hand page, her thoughts. The fold between these two sets of pages makes evident the use, on the left pages, of a metalanguage. Contrary to the title, there is no intertwining here.
27 Jacques Lacan, *Le champ freudien* (Paris, Éditions du Seuil, 1968, p. 9). Jean Allouch, *Exposé sur Nouvelles remarques sur le passage à l'acte* (14 December 2019, p. 11).
28 Jacques Lacan, *Écrits* (Paris, Éditions du Seuil, 1966, p. 430).
29 Fernando Pessoa, *Livre(s) de l'inquiétude*, translated from Portuguese by Marie-Hélène Piwnik (Paris, Bourgeois, p. 233).
30 Due to Lacan, this neologism was waiting to take shape, or better, flesh. In *La Scène lacanienne et son cercle magique* (Paris, Epel, 2017), it is Erri de Luca that I relied on to do this, playing once again on this proximity of madness and literature so well recognised and clarified by Michel Foucault.
31 Hence my proposal to change "psychoanalysis" to "spichanalysis" (*Is psychoanalysis a spiritual exercise? Response to Michel Foucault*, Paris, Epel, 2007).

Provenance of Texts

Included in the Introduction are the remarks for the place and function of historical narrative in psychoanalysis, which was first presented during a seminar held in Montevideo, Uruguay, 28–29 July 2018. Presented at the same seminar was the discussion of the enlightened passage to the act, as it is in the Conclusion of the present book.

Chapter I was partly written following a seminar in Rosario, Argentina, 21–22 April 2018.

Some elements of Chapters II and III were the subject of a presentation during a conference entitled, "Saut épique et passage à l'acte", held by *l'École lacanienne de psychanalyse*, Paris, 3 February 2018, at which Fethi Benslama also spoke.

Chapter II, "To think, to act: Louis Althusser", was first presented during the colloquium, 1 July 2018, entitled "Louis Althusser: politique, philosophie", held at Centre Culturel International de Cerisy-la-Salle, under the direction of Bertrand Ogilvie and Julia Christ.

Acknowledgements

It so happens that friendship in no way blunts critical acuity. Once again, Isabelle Châtelet, Guy Le Gaufrey, Thierry Marchaissse and Mayette Viltard have proved this to be true. For this, I thank them.

Introduction

Just a moment, wait, you who have begun to read me ... Rather than going further into these pages, go onto the Internet for just a few minutes. There, a choreography awaits you: it will plunge you into a pool, the same one as this book. We owe it to Clément Cogitore. He, along with three choreographers, Bintou Dembele, Igor Caruge and Brahim Rachiki, invited a group of Krump dancers to display their talents in the "Air de Sauvages" of Rameau's opera, the *Indes galantes*. Krump originated in the late 1990s in the poor areas of Los Angeles. "Krump", the acronym for "Kingdom Radically Uplifted Mighty Praise", is the dance of uprising.[1]

By way of preamble, let us not stop there. After dance, there is sporting performance. It casts a valuable light on the way in which thought or, rather, "thinking" can only be absent when the act occurs. Thomas Diet was the world vice-champion of free-ride skiing: a discipline in which speed carries the beautiful name of "fluidity". His motto, "To reflect is to capitulate",[2] explains what he does at the moment that he launches himself and then accomplishes a descent during which he jumps down impressive rock faces, risking severe injury and, indeed, his life. To no longer think, to not think: this is a necessary condition in order for his descent to be successful. Beforehand, of course, he would have carefully studied the terrain and examined the different conditions that he would confront during his descent – the snow conditions, the trace of his momentum, the sheer faces, the soft landing places. It's called "reading the line of descent", in the same way that surfers "read" the waves. However, the "acting" itself demands the absence of all thought, especially in individual sports. According to Henry Kissinger, whoever conquers power – "that ultimate aphrodisiac" – ceases to think. This lesson is worthwhile for the analyst – who we will consider, in what follows, without allowing thought, albeit unconscious, to fill all the space of questioning and of analytical practice.

Among all the phenomena that are the objects of psychiatric discourse and practices, there is one that may be distinguished due to its position at the intersection of at least four different registers. Distinct, in this, from symptom, inhibition and anxiety (the Freudian ternary), the passage to the act is relevant to the psychiatric, the judicial, the political[3] and, let us say, the sociocultural.

DOI: 10.4324/9781003504092-1

One only has to consider the Papin sisters to no longer have any doubt about this.[4] And it would doubtless be advisable to see in this, rather than a case, a "Papin affair" – the crime that is never extinguished, an incandescent fire. A passage to the act concerns the whole of society. This is made most obvious by the media as the most salient emergent point of madness and psychiatry in the social domain. Driven to leave its sphere, psychiatric discourse finds itself confronted by more legitimate difficulties than those treated within it. The problems that beset it become noteworthy, and we no longer know who is in a position to resolve them. Is the public at large – and no longer just specialists – expected to deal with them, in spite of lacking the means to do so?

Relevant in this context are the audiences who have viewed Raymond Depardon's film, *Twelve Days*, which is as gripping as it is instructive. The film is about the legal time limit imposed by French law regarding a patient subjected to involuntary psychiatric hospitalisation. The patient must appear before a liberty and custody judge, who must decide whether the patient should remain in hospital or be free to leave. Depardon documented and filmed some of these cases conducted in the Vinatier Psychiatric Hospital in Lyon. Among the many remarkable details, what is striking is that the decisions of the psychiatric experts and then of the judges are influenced by an obsession with regard to the nine detainees being judged. This obsession is the dread of the passage to the act, which must be avoided at all costs. But is a fear of this kind likely to result in the best approach to the passage to the act? I think this is doubtful.

Due to Marcel Mauss,[5] the concept of a "total social fact" seems to suit the passage to the act. More simply, perhaps, the passage to the act could be qualified as an event that does not "do the trick" [*fait l'affaire*] but nevertheless "does the job" [*fait affaire*]. As a consequence of this status, there comes the way in which we propose, right here, to treat the passage to the act, not so much under the aegis of psychiatric or psychoanalytical practice and theory, but rather with reference to several means of expression: cinema, literature, the media, etc. Notably, the following will be addressed: the acts of the jihadist, of Louis Althusser and of Claire Lannes, the protagonist of Marguerite Duras' novel, *L'Amante anglaise*.

Consider the generic term "event". Some events allow themselves to be easily inscribed in what we may call a history and, as far as the practice of analysis is concerned, a life history. Such events are not all that unusual in this history: they take their place in it (at least, that is what one thinks initially), whether from the point of view of the agent (we will return to this point) or from that of those who have been attacked, interested, touched or troubled by them. But other events do not allow themselves to fit into a history, into a story. We don't know where they come from, what they refer to, or what could have set them off. They seem to come from nowhere and to go nowhere. They are non-sensical and do not lend themselves to be contextualised. What comes to mind immediately is the symptom, as it has been redefined by psychoanalysis. We can also evoke events that present themselves as extremes: on the one hand, the incomprehensible crime of the Papin sisters and, on the other, making sense, the reassignment surgery of the transsexual, the jihadist attack, or even the act of the suttee who immolates herself on her husband's funeral pyre, although not without leaving a trace – the trace of her hand at the entrance of the conjugal home,[6] just as the jihadists of 11 September 2001 left a trace in the form of a signed text, which was reported not long afterwards by *Le Monde* (see Chapter I).

This distributive criterion is nothing new, but rather a Lacanian relic. What is new here is the application that will be developed from it: notably, from the fact that was recently proposed by Fethi Benslama, the "epic leap," which he specified, named and described – that is, a particular way of "resorting to violence", which stands as a stumbling block to the "paradigm of mental illness" (*Libération*, 12 October 2017). Invited by L'École lacanienne on 3 February 2018, Benslama delineated more clearly the extent of his discovery, much more than the possibilities offered to him by the media platform of a daily newspaper. We thus learned that the term itself, "epic leap", came to him while he was in Tunisia in 2011 and witnessed the people's uprising. I recently used the term "uprising" differently to "epic leap", having received it from Michel Foucault who characterised another "revolution" in this way: the Iranian revolution.[7] Nonetheless, these different choices have not prevented me from welcoming the discovery of the epic leap and from using it, as it is evident in this work. Benslama draws attention to the epic (*Mahabharata, The Odyssey, The Aeneid, Gilgamesh, The Legend of the Ages*) as associated with other modalities of stories in the West: tragic, dramatic and comic. He also indicates that the epic, which entered the Freudian field with Otto Rank,[8] is discreetly present in Lacan – for the first time when he made the epic an equivalent of verbalisation, for a second time when he turned the myth into the objectified representation of an *epos*, the function of which coincides the experience of a neurotic.[9]

Here we will consider the epic leap according to one of the two definitions, which are nonetheless linked, that Benslama presented on 3 February 2019. The first and more extensive definition situates the epic leap as "the moment when the movement of a *separation* of what someone was, so that a break or bifurcation is brought about in his existential trajectory, a break from which he then adopts an *agonistic* way of appearing, speaking and acting".[10] We can approach the second and more restrained definition of the epic leap by citing the testament of a jihadist candidate for martyrdom, mentioned by Benslama: "My brothers, I have sworn to present myself to God and my master, Imam Hussein, only in small pieces, without head and hands, in order to possess real merit before the king of kings and before Imam Hussein."[11] While this way of epic leap is in line with the first, it nonetheless can be distinguished from it in a similar way to what happened to Paul of Tarsus on the road to Damascus (the adoption of a new war in the Antipodes, to the one carried out before) and the act of the crusaders going to Palestine to massacre the impious who did not want to convert. Benslama indicated the difference between these two modalities of the epic leap by immediately and rightly refusing to recognise a passage to the act in the break whereby someone becomes violent and engages in jihadism: a change that does not in any way make him a waste product. Whilst he admits that in his sacrifice, whoever has read his testament "lets his body fall like waste", would this, nonetheless, be a passage to the act? We will rather consider this gesture as an "epic leap", because it allows itself to be easily inscribed in an epic story, a story that makes sense. Jihadists, people have said and still continue to say, "pass to the act". The fortunate discovery of the epic leap evoked in the restricted sense that has just been described invites us to consider, afresh, what is understood as the "passage to the act".

Before correcting himself, Lacan strongly put forward the criterion of what does or does not make sense. In 1953, he defined the unconscious as "the chapter of my history that is signed by a blank or occupied by a lie: it's the censored chapter".[12] We also read:

> It is indeed the subject's assumption of his history, insofar as it consists by speech addressed to the other,[13] which creates the foundation of what Freud named psychoanalysis.

And, four years later:

> This is the truth of what desire was in its history: that the subject cries through his symptom, as Christ said that the stones would cry if the children of Israel had not given them voice.[14]

Two mishaps have struck this recourse to meaning and history – indeed, to the meaning of a history. It happens to have been adopted by current discourse even though Lacan expressed serious reservations about it.

Here, then, is the criterion of a historicised meaning (a signification, an orientation) that, in particular, discriminates the epic leap (carrier of meaning) from the passage to the act (outside meaning). This kind of distinction occurs elsewhere. Symptom, parapraxis and dream also pertain to the act, insofar as *the act cannot be reabsorbed by, and in, meaning*. A symptom, a dream, a parapraxis take place outside history and are manifested rather like a spreadsheet in a Zen garden or a pig in a synagogue.[15] Exemplary in this regard is a clinical note by Lacan. There was someone who carefully arranged his shoes in precisely the same place every night before going to bed and who, anxious, could not fall asleep if he had forgotten this nightly homage to his shoes. One day, he felt astonished by this, and it was only at that moment, remarked Lacan, that the symptom was fully constituted, because of the fact that it then seemed to neither have any connection to his history nor any sense.

Many efforts are made (at times, undergoing a psychoanalysis) to scribble this page with a text – this page, the whiteness of which is made present by the symptom – and to attempt to bring this kind of ahistoric event back into the centre of a historical narrative to make it look coherent. Nonetheless, the interpretation remains without any grip on the act itself, which in different ways constitutes the symptom, the dream or the parapraxis. Thus, returning again to the symptom that we have just described, could any of this man's acquaintances consider this behaviour as being bizarre, if not inaccessible, metamorphised as he has been into a stranger by the symptom? One of the facets of the act of the symptom, which no interpretation can ever resorb, has to do with it having an effect in the other.

The emphasis that Lacan placed so squarely on alterity should have led to the symptom being envisaged by no longer asking what could have caused it, in the subject in which it is a parasite, but by asking about its effect on the person's entourage – the entourage to which the analyst belongs as soon as an analysis begins? Exemplary in this regard is another clinical observation of Lacan's, according to which so-called melancholy is a moral fault. Who could doubt for a moment the negative effect that melancholic laments and other suicidal ideas have on those around the person who is dripping with anxiety? Who could doubt the pernicious consequences of an inhibition? Or the setbacks in the erotic, no matter what order of impulse they may be? To no longer envisage inhibition, anxiety and the symptom by tracking down their origin in the analysand (this is what the prejudice of psychology, of the "psy function", consists of), but through their effect on the other is, precisely, what the transference invites, the path that it opens. Where, for instance, anxiety causes anxiety to someone close to the anxious person, the analyst – who is himself sensitive to this kind of overflow, being pervious himself – would know, unlike someone else in the person's entourage, how to mop it up: at least in the sense that he will silence in the analysis his own anxiety, which has thus been evoked. A wonderful work to pursue, following on from the work of Marco Decorpeliada,[16] would be to take up ironically the whole of so-called psychopathology and to rewrite it – no longer from its own viewpoint, which considers the patient as both an agent and an object, but according to the effects that the patient's symptoms, inhibitions and anxieties have on his or her entourage. Isn't the transference the royal road that the symptom goes down to eventually fade away? And its disappearance is not even noticed until after it has happened. Let us begin by indicating that, 20 years later, Lacan would not have taken up, just as it was, his positioning of the unconscious through reference to history. The latter even ended up grating on him. Nonetheless, history is far from being absent from the sayings of the analysand and, in this, the analyst could not prove him wrong either. However, does this affirm – as is still written today – that an analysis concludes by offering the analysand a coherent narrative of his life, as Lacan put in the 1950s?[17]

Two remarks in this regard. (1) In analysis, the act puts it seal on several notions: passage to the act, parapraxis, acting out, sexual act and analytic act. So far, I haven't come across any study of this fragmentation of the act, any study that asks whether, in these different instantiations, the term "act" remains marked by the same trait, which could alone justify its use here and there. Such a trait could be called "actuality". Or, on the contrary, does "act" present in all these different occurrences such different meanings that its diversified use has no other effect than to give rise to confusion?

(2) Each of the *"formations of the unconscious"* (the name given to them by Lacan) refer to the act – which does not in any way mean that there is no act outside of the manifestation of these formations. Relevant here is something that Freud said. Ostracised from Vienna, the famous Freud arrived to live in London. The BBC contacted him, hoping for an interview. The request was precise: they wanted to know what he thought of recent events and what had happened to make the Nazis cause him to leave his beloved city, Vienna. Freud's response: he would not say anything about that but would accept to be interviewed if the interviewer would stick to asking him about psychoanalysis. It was the same with Zinédine Zidane when he had reached the pinnacle of his career. He was asked about some political event or other. His response: "Ask me about football." For these two situations, the act of cutting-off defined a field that, without the cutting act, would have dissolved into the shifting sands of current and general discourse. In this regard, we recall a position taken by Michel Foucault that some could consider to be rudeness, plain and simple. In the early 1960s, he was invited by the School of Criminology at the University of Montreal, directed by Denis Szabo (from whom the following story was obtained[18]). The School wanted to ensure that Foucault was given the best possible conditions in order to complete *Surveiller et punir. Naissance de la prison.*[19] Attentive to the rules of hospitality, accompanied by his wife, Szabo invited his guest out to eat and to chat ... not more than two or three times. Anyhow, here is how, as quoted by Szabo, Foucault put an end to these occasions:

> "Listen, it's a pleasure for me to listen to you and to converse with you but, if you permit me, let's leave it at that. I am here to finish a book. My time is extremely limited, and above all, I want to prove a thesis." He literally said this to me. "Listening to you, I will never finish because there's this, and there's that, and other things. I don't have the time to go chasing all these rabbits; I don't have time to verify all this." And I'll never forget his final words: "I want to remain in a state of creative ignorance. And with you, in this environment, this isn't possible." I never saw him again.

While in other places *the passion for ignoranc*e can be nourished, here, the act of cutting-off allows for *"creative ignorance"* and even seems to be its condition of possibility.

Now, let us consider the case of the (*parapraxis*) failed act: Lacan asked himself whether it consisted of one "facet of the act".[20] And this is, indeed how it is, and this is the reason that Freud, rather than limiting himself to only the clumsiness of certain gestures, put forward his *Fehlleistung, the failed act*, translated into French as "*l'acte manqué*", which emphasises the "facet of the act" just as the Spanish translation (*acto fallido*), Italian translation (*atto mancato*) and Portuguese translation (*ato falho* or *perturbado*) do, whereas with the term *parapraxis*, English speakers efface the act somewhat, even though *praxis* means "action" [in Greek]. In a recent article, Thomas Elsaesser, a professor at the University of Amsterdam, wrote: "In German, the compound *Fehlleistung* is contradictory because *fehl* means 'failed' or 'absent' and *Leistung* means 'performance'."[21] On the contrary, analysis values the apparent "contradiction" in recognising the failed performance as succeeded.

Consider someone whose friends have invited him for dinner. A clumsy movement causes him to break the glass of wine he's been offered. Any Freudian would think that this unfortunate act, which creates a moment of disturbance or embarrassment in the company, carries a message that may or may not be deciphered then and there or later on. So, for example, the host may have said something that, for the breaker of the glass, caused disapproval that was not expressed but instead manifested in the form of the breaking of the glass. An alert ear would hear the phrase, "Let's break it off here", a way of ending a conversation (and here, yes, we can speak not of a "passage to the act" but of a *passage through the act* of the unexpressed disapproval). Nonetheless, although the failed act will have been interpreted, the glass will remain broken, and the host will have to buy another one. Here we have one of the faces of the act of the failed act. As an act, it finds itself without any possible return onto itself: it cannot be undone, made up for or annulled. Contrary to the signifier conceived as the effacement of the trace,[22] the act cannot be effaced. It can rebound, give rise to a re-act, to a reaction, but this reaction will not annul the act.

The lapsus is about speech, In *The Psychopathology of Everyday Life*, Freud distinguishes, out of thousands of examples, the case of "self-betrayal by lapsus".[23] Here we have the auto-betrayal of an anatomist: "As far as the female genital organs are concerned, we have, in spite of many *temptations* [*tentations*]... sorry, many *attempts* [*tentatives*] ..."[24] And also, Freud's patient, to whom he had just pointed out that she was ashamed of her family and had made a reproach to her father, "the substance of which we[25] still do not know". The patient immediately stated that Freud's comment was improbable but continued: "One must nonetheless acknowledge one thing about them: they are really people who are set apart. They all have a great *finance of mind* [*finance d'esprit*] ... I mean, a great *fineness of mind* [*finesse d'esprit*]."[26] In both examples, the shot was fired – such a premature (e)jaculation of words. Even though it was not wanted, it was said, and allows no means of going back.

After the failed act and the lapsus, we acknowledge the dream as an event that has the status of being an act. The best proof of this is Freud's brief remark that the most successful dream is the dream of which one has no memory. Here, Freud is distancing himself from the *Talmud*, which stated that "a non-interpreted dream is like an unread letter". Furthermore, the discovery of the dream's *navel* also clearly signals the facet of the act of the dream that remains excluded from interpretation, from *Deutung*, from meaning, from narrative. The dream reaching this umbilical point, where interpretation finds its limit, has the significance of an event.

Several historical circumstances led Lacan (his rejection of history) and some Lacanians thereafter (fascinated by the signifier) to abandon – without even knowing it – the narrative in the hands of Paul Ricœur. We still have not estimated the extent to which this neglect has been a disaster. The discovery of the epic leap in the place where the passage to the act is evoked is utterly connected to the narrative and obliges us to get back to work on what we have known so far concerning the passage to the act.

This is the task of this book. [*Translator's note*: A recent book by Fintan O'Toole, *Shakespeare is hard, but so is life*, published in 2024, deals with similar problems and difficulties in the field of literature to those that Allouch confronts with this book in the field of psychoanalysis. According to O'Toole, both fields are full of misleading simplifications and useless moral rules, like standard studies of Shakespeare.] Here, we will see the notion of the passage to the act being gradually broken in order to give way to, and find itself transformed not simply to the epic leap, but also to the play (in the sense that two "play" in relation to each other) between this newly defined passage to the act and the epic leap. With Louis Althusser, the murderer of Hélène Rytman (see Chapter II), we will be led to no longer envisage his action as a single piece. Without being able to clearly distinguish the co-presence of an epic leap and a passage to the act, the latter cannot be understood as a whole; because two "*Comes*" co-exist: the first addressed to Hélène, who could be rendered present and loving only as dead; the second, where she was a support, being a vain attempt to make the sexual relation, the Other or still God, to exist.

In contrast, the distinction between the passage to the act and the epic leap appears clearly with the murder of Marie-Thérèse Bousquet committed by Claire Lannes (see Chapter III, devoted to *L'Amante anglaise*). The passage to the act here is held in one word: "vomit", vomit the meat in sauce that Marie-Thérèse had become, while the epic leap that accompanies it presents itself in the form of a letter addressed to a former lover that the murderer has never stopped loving. He also was a support likely to make the Other and the sexual relation exist, and God with them. Substantiated twice here, is Lacan's statement that "the true formula of atheism, is that God is unconscious".[27]

From there, we find ourselves more capable of – if not grasping – at least perceiving more closely (in conclusion) what Jacques Lacan could have had in mind in inviting the analyst to abide by the "I do not think", characteristic of the passage to the act. A passage to the act that is rather strange, even teratological: at least at first sight, as soon as it is qualified as "notified" or as "clarified". Therefore, the crucial question at the end of an analysis and the different question of the passage of the analysand to analyst must be reconsidered. We will show that, in this place, the distinction between the passage to the act and the epic leap proves to be heuristic. It is by means of an epic leap that an analysis ends, an epic leap that puts the analysand in a position of readiness to achieve the clarified passage to the act that establishes him or her as analyst, capable of not thinking.

"To not think": this phrase suits being the last in this introduction.

Notes

1 https://www.youtube.com/watch?v=9h9HP-VOJv4. See also the interview with Clément Cogitore on YouTube, as well as M.-Ch. Vernay's article in *Libération*, 14 May 2013.
2 Thomas Diet lost his life in a car accident on 16 March 2019. The online review, *Skieur Magazine*, rendered homage to him by republishing a 2005 interview giving the context of his motto, "To reflect is to capitulate".
3 As in Nicolas Sarkozy bringing in a liberticidal law, privileging safety over care, not long after a student in Grenoble was killed by a so-called psychiatric patient.
4 Jacques Lacan published his article on the Papin sisters in a surrealist review. See Francis Dupré, *La "Solution" du passage à l'acte. Le double crime des sœurs Papin* (Toulouse, Érès, 1984).
5 Marcel Mauss, "Essai sur le don. Forme et raison de l'échange dans les sociétés primitives", *L'Année sociologique* (2nd series), 1923–1924 (cited in *Sociologie et anthropologie*, Presses universitaires de France, collection "Quadrige", 1968 and 1973).
6 Catherine Weinberger-Thomas, *Cendres d'immortalité. La crémation des veuves en Inde* (Paris, Éditions du Seuil, 1996).
7 Jean Allouch, *La Scène lacanienne et son cercle magique. Des fous se soulèvent* (Paris, Epel, 2017).
8 Otto Rank, *Le Mythe de la naissance du héros* [1909] (Paris, Payot, 2000).
9 In "Fonction et champ de la parole et du langage en Psychanalyse" (Jacques Lacan, *Écrits*, Éditions du Seuil, Paris, 1966, p. 237) and "Le mythe individuel du névrosé" respectively, 1953 (see https://www.freud-lacan.com/).
10 Fethi Benslama, "Le saut épique", *L'École lacanienne de psychanalyse* (Paris, 3 February 2018). Unpublished. Benslama's italics.
11 Fethi Benslama first mentioned this text in *La Guerre des subjectivités en islam* (Paris, Éditions Lignes, 2014, p. 86).
12 Jacques Lacan, "Fonction et champ de parole et du langage" [1953], in *Écrits* (Paris, Éditions du Seuil, 1966, p. 257).
13 We would expect "*l'Autre*". But, above all, this is a statement in which it would be judicious to write "*otre*" (both "*autre*" and "*Autre*") – which is what I proposed at the time.
14 Jacques Lacan, "L'instance de la lettre dans l'inconscient ou la raison depuis Freud", in *Écrits* (Paris, Éditions du Seuil, 1966, p. 519).
15 A horrific image, conveyed in Matan Yair's film, *Les Destinées d'Asher* (2017).
16 Marco Decorpeliada, *Schizomètre. Petit manuel de survie en milieu psychiatrique* (Paris, Epel, 2010); Benoît Vidal, *L'Effet schizomètre* (Paris, Epel, 2018).
17 "It is the assumption by the subject of his history, insofar as it is constituted by speech addressed to the other, that is the foundation of the new method that Freud

has named psychoanalysis" (Jacques Lacan, "Fonction et champ de la parole et du langage", *Écrits* (Paris, Éditions du Seuil, 1966, p. 257). A page earlier, he referred to "the intersubjective continuity of the discourse in which the history of the subject is constituted".

18 On my part [Allouch] heard the story from Guy Casadamont, who spoke of it during the Colloque "Après Les Aveux de la chair, Généalogy du sujet, Généalogy de la Psychanalyse chez Michel Foucault" (Université Paris 7-Diderot, Parisles, 18 and 19 January 2019).
19 Michel Foucault, *Surveiller et punir, Naissance de la prison* (Paris, Gallimard, 1975).
20 Jacques Lacan, Seminar, *L'Acte psychanalytique*, 22 November 1967.
21 Thomas Elsaesser, "Cent mille hasards qu'après coup on appelle destin", translated from German by Céline Letawe, *Cahiers d'études germaniques*, No. 69, 2015 (consulted online 17 December 2017).
22 See my presentation of this effacement in Jean Allouch, *Lettre pour lettre. Transcrire, traduire, translittérer* (Toulouse, Érès, 1984, pp. 165, 232 and 317).
23 Sigmund Freud, *Psychologie de la vie quotidienne*, translated from German by Denis Messier, Preface by Laurence Kahn (Paris, Gallimard, 1977, p. 163).
24 Sigmund Freud, *Psychologie de la vie quotidienne*, translated from German by Denis Messier, Preface by Laurence Kahn (Paris, Gallimard, 1977, p. 149). Note that the edition signals that the signifying proximity is no less present in German: *Versuchungen* ("*tentations*") and *Versuche* ("*tentatives*").
25 Who then, is this "we"? The royal "we"? Or does it indicate what has been called a "therapeutic alliance with the patient", a bias that Lacan removed from analytic practice? On the subject of this "we" that, unmistakably, indicates that there are those who are not part of the family, nation, group or community who we call "they", we refer to two pages of Philip Roth's novel, *The Human Stain* [*La Tache*, translated from English by Josée Kamoun (Paris, Gallimard, 2000, pp. 139–140)], where he emphasises the segregative significance of "we", as well as its coercive nature as an assimilator of all singularity. "We" is a wall. "We" comforts and fixes in place the narcissism of each person living behind the shelter of this wall. Following on from Freud's remark that the ideal of the "I" has a social side, Norbert Elias invented the "ideal of we", conceived as a determined stratum of the ideal of the "I", the idealised state of an "I" who says "we" (Norbert Elias, *Logiques de l'exclusion*, Paris, Fayard, 1997). A simple toothache is enough to stop "we" from prevailing.
26 Sigmund Freud, *Psychologie de la vie quotidienne* (Paris, Gallimard, 1977, p. 149) *Der Geist:* "mind"; *der Geiz*: "greed".
27 Jacques Lacan, *Les Quatre concepts fondamentaux de la psychanalyse* (Paris, Éditions du Seuil, 1973, p. 58).

Chapter I

Actuality of the passage to the act

Experts

On 12 May 2017, *Le Monde* published an article entitled, "It is futile to try to provide a clear logic about the passage to the act". The text was about two psychiatric experts on the so-called "poisoner of Chambéry", a nurse who had killed several old people in the retirement home where she worked because, she said, she wanted "to do them good". The details of the events reported in the paper as well as of "the poisoner's" personality matter little here. Rather, we should consider the expert opinions as reported by *Le Monde* because they are typical of the way in which people usually think of the passage to the act.

While this woman admitted to the facts, we read, she seemed "incapable of answering this question: why?". However, is this the question that should have been asked of the accused? Science can attempt to clarify the question, "How did this happen?" but abstains from asking, "Why did this happen?". Imagine for a moment that someone asks you, out of the blue, *why* you made a particular important decision – for example, having a child. Could you answer? For me, even though I have explored thousands of answers to similar questions, I have had to admit that they all disappear like so many bubbles blown into the air by a public entertainer. I have thus found myself incapable of answering, even after many years of analysis … or, rather, thanks to many years of analysis.

In what terms do these experts speak of the accused? They use a vocabulary of their own, without any regard for the literality of the words that are heard, which refer only to meanings that are supposed to be picked up without any loss or malformation. It is suggested that this transposition takes into account what was read or heard. They present the "poisoner" as a "vulnerable", "immature", "split" personality with an "impaired judgement", "dependent on an over-protective mother"; the said personality "collapsed" following the death of this mother; they use the word "disavowal"; they see in the passage to the act an "impulsive discharge". Having been present at the hearing, Henri Sekel, journalist at *Le Monde*, writes:

> This sums up a day during which jargon and several abstruse explanations often plunged the audience into the depths of perplexity. How many of the

jurors (and magistrates, civil parties and journalists) had already heard of concepts like "anaclitic relation", "introjection" or "destructivity"? It was not clear at all and did not provide any answers.

There is an abysmal contrast with Freud's discourse, who could be heard and read by the so-called "honest man". In the end, these experts saved themselves from the quagmire they had got themselves into by their statement that they could not "provide a clear logic to the passage to the act". But, then, why this jargon? Do people *jargonise* all the more when they don't know that they're doing so?

Here, as in several psychoanalytical publications, there is a particular use of knowledge that, in other areas, has been rightly discarded. Thus, for example, the notion of the "myth" has recently appeared without corresponding to, but rather distorting, what the ancient Greeks meant by "*mûthos*". The same is true of "*logos*" which has, moreover, been artificially opposed to *mûtho* in the belief that they are inherently opposites. For many years now, a whole movement has taken off in the perception that the European intellectuals of the nineteenth and twentieth centuries projected onto the texts they studied (in Sanskrit, Greek, etc.) categories that had no equivalents in the texts themselves. We have got rid of a kind of colonialism of thought, a welcome and fertile enterprise, to which John Winkler, Edward Said, Marcel Detienne and, more recently, Claude Calame, Philippe Descola, Sandra Boehringer and Michel Angot[1] have all contributed. (This list is arbitrary and not meant to be exhaustive.) It does not seem, however, that the majority of psychoanalysts have devoted themselves to this enterprise.

Five months later (20 October 2017), *Le Monde* gave the title "There is a new jouissance of hatred" ("*Il y a une jouissance nouvelle de la haine*") to an interview with a philosopher and a psychoanalyst. "New" with regard to which former jouissance(s)? "New" in what sense? One is at once struck – and baffled – by this punchy title. Question: "Have you witnessed in your patients the emergence of an unprecedented hatred?" Response, tolerating no doubt whatsoever: "Absolutely. There is a new jouissance of hatred, which is problematic as it somehow justifies the passage to the act".[2] And, further on whoever passes to the act topples into "the evil side, that of destruction". The interviewee then adds: "In these kinds of conversions, it is subjectivity that is abolished." No less! Go and tell this to those who destroyed the Twin Towers (we'll get to this). No more subject but, all the same, a good side and an evil side. Is this a psychoanalytic way of thinking? Can the passage to the act be located in what, for centuries, has been called "Evil" or the "Devil"? Passing to the act is evil.

This was confirmed for me in the following manner. A Jacques Lacan Symposium was held in Vienna on 9 June 2001 (he would have been 100 years old), which selected as its theme the passage to the act. I had given my talk the title "The badly named passage to the act" (*Le mal nommé passage à l'acte*).

What did my translator into German read? Without noticing, he introduced, indeed hallucinated, a comma between "le mal" and "nommé" and thus announced my talk "*Le mal, nommé passage à l'acte*" ("Evil/Bad, named the passage to the act"), whereas I was indicating that the passage to the act was a nomination that did not suit its object (the reasons will be given below). This translator merely took upon himself the most common thought about the passage to the act, so I couldn't really reproach him for it.

Good can counteract this evil, according to the expert on the passage to the act, consulted by *Le Monde*. "Something must be woven into the language side," she goes on, "which will allow the act to be suspended, which will repress the hate-filled impulse." Her solution, which can be seen in the sort of power she accords to weaving and language, is "Lacanian". Hatred is supposed to destroy discourse. As if no discourse of hatred exists (André Gide: "Family, I hate you! Closed homes, closed doors; possessions jealous of happiness"), one should, by speaking, reintegrate hatred into language, which will make it "value its rights" – does language as such, then, have rights? These statements are miles away from the passage to the act, and I would not be interested in them if they did not convey a largely accepted conception of the passage to the act. Which one?

The conception is inconveniently magnified by the expression itself: "passage to the act". "Passage" suggests that a certain assertion is already there, like the relay baton passed from hand to hand in a four by hundred metre relay, in some form or other, in whoever – *instead of* carrying it to words – carries it to the act. This act, therefore, could have not been committed.

This was the conception of the passage to the act suggested by Lacan when he first revised the case [Freud's case] of the "young homosexual woman" ("The psychogenesis of a case of homosexuality in a woman"). The equivocation of *niederkommen* (meaning both "to fall down" and "to give birth") initially played a nasty trick on the Lacanian conception of the passage to the act. In 1956–1957, this signifying equivocation pushed Lacan to present her jump over a wall, down the side of a cutting and onto a railway line as a "symbolic act": in letting herself fall, the young woman was supposedly manifesting her desire to give birth to a child by her father. Extending a movement initiated by Lacan, I put to the sword this, in part, blatantly false version. Freud had already given Margarethe Csonka[3] many reasons to laugh and be scornful of him.

This version was then all the more accepted as Freud observed that an element of the order of language could not occur in speech (to be "worked through") but it could manifest itself in what he then called *agieren*. In "Remembering, repeating and working-through", published in 1914, he wrote:

> The analysand does not remembered anything of what he has forgotten and repressed, but he <u>acts</u> (*agiere*). He does not reproduce (*reproduziert*) it as a memory but, on the contrary, as act (<u>Tat</u>) and he *repeats* it without, of course, knowing that he is repeating it.[4]

Here dwells indeed the disparity between these two registers (that of remembering and that of the act), which Wittgenstein so clearly revealed (the disparity, for him, between saying and doing). Nonetheless, the Freudian term was not "passage to the act" but *agieren*, translated into English as "acting-out", which [in turn] was seen by Lacan as a "wild transference" or as "transference without analysis". Acting-out has a trait in common with transference that specifies each of them: acting-out aims to be a monstration that appeals to interpretation.[5] There is no possibility of interpretation without a *passage* of a certain text (that the subject does not remember) coming to the scene of the acting-out. Having thus discussed the passage to the act during the course of the seminar, *La Relation d'objet* (1956–1957), Lacan envisaged the young homosexual woman's passage to the act as different to a "symbolic act."[6] Even later, in putting forward the psychoanalytic act (in his interrupted seminar of 1967–1968), *he made the act incommensurable with the symbolic*. Different to the (*agieren*) as Freud presented it, the passage to the act is not at all a *passage*, but rather the tangible manifestation and attempt to resolve an impasse.

Drowning, fragmentation and condemnation of the passage to the act

In 2013, the international review, *La Clinique lacanienne*,[7] devoted a collection (11 contributions) on the chosen theme: "Passage to the act" (*Passer à l'acte*). Upon reading these 115 pages, what is striking is that, apart from one mention with no development, none of the passages to the act studied by Lacan are the object of any remarks at all: not the one of the Papin sisters, not Marguerite Anzieu's and not the one of the so-called "young homosexual woman". As for other passages to the act that are well-known and discussed in psychiatry – there is nothing about them either. One begins to glimpse one of the motives for this impasse when one reads the question that is posed on the back cover, "How can the passage to the act of patients be managed?". Here we have Lacanian psychoanalysts becoming managers, while those designated as analysands[8] by Lacan are once again given their former status as patients. One then wonders whether, apart from a time when no one "managed their relationship", Jacques Lacan may not have his quota of responsibility in what is claimed to be from him, and yet turns away from him even while speaking Lacanian.

"To manage": what is meant here above all else is "to avoid" because the concern that was noted with regard to the experts' discourse at the beginning of this chapter is still dominant here. Here too, the conception that, through speaking, it would be possible to obtain from the "patient" – for his own greater good – that he will abstain from passing to the act (for example, p. 79, p. 86 and p. 89,[9] as well as p. 109,[10] p. 111, p. 114, p. 116[11]). Also present here, furthermore, and linked to this conception, is the idea that there is something that changes register, that "passes" to the act and ought not to (for example, p. 51).

In this volume, the absence of such particular events that have been distinguished and qualified as passages to the act does not arise from simple negligence. The comments made by the contributors are put into the service of an intention, which may be unknown, but which can be formulated thus: to drown the fish (*noyer le poisson*) of the passage to the act, seen as venom ("*poison*"). [*Translator's note*: The proverb *noyer le poisson* means something alike to avoid the issue or sidestep the question.] However, it is not all that easy to drown a fish. To multiply the quotations that attest to this drowning would be so easy that we prefer to mention just three. Confusion is created by the statement (p. 35) that "the notion of the passage to the act" is what gives its title to the seminar, *L'Acte analytique*.¹² Confusion is also created by mixing (p. 111) the passage to the act and the act of speaking in the following formula: "passage to the ordinary act of speaking". Ordinary? Who doesn't know that, when someone begins to speak, there is nothing ordinary in this?¹³ The same contributor, who sees a passage to the act in the sexual act (p. 115), clearly states (on the same page) the disappearance of the passage to the act in what it has specifically: "*As we have seen, the passage to the act therefore has a vast domain of extension*".

This evacuation of the passage to the act gives rise to and even allows two affirmations – which are, moreover, correlated – to be put forward: a claim and a condemnation. What can be qualified as a "claim" is the promotion of the psychoanalytic act, coming in a straight line from Lacan but presented in a completely different tonality from the one that is applied here. The "new deal" Lacanian psychoanalyst, a performer, a champion, is presented as someone who, on the one hand, *knows* what the passage to the act consists of (p. 106, and also p. 93 and p. 96) and who, at the same time, would be likely to carry out his work according to the watchword "to pass to the act". His act is proclaimed at once as risky and dignified:¹⁴ he is to raise "the individual submitted to an insidious jouissance to the dimension of a subject who takes full responsibility as an agent of a reworked jouissance" and who would thus pass from an illusory satisfaction to other satisfaction (pp. 9–10). Has anyone done better in terms of promising the shining tomorrows sung at Sunday services?

With regard to the analytic act, Lacan's tone was definitely not like this. He wondered whether announcing that the end of an analysis is, on the part of the analysand, a "subjective destitution" would make potential analysands flee. Neither did he see any dignity in what is correspondingly produced on the part of the analyst: what he called "un-being" ("*désêtre*"). Shall we go and look further into what he said? His term, "*déchariter*"¹⁵ [a combination of *déchet* and *charité* = waste and charity], by which he characterised the position of the analyst as lacking of any dignity, and devoid of any promise.

The Lacanian pastoral that we have just evoked, while commenting on Lacan, is committed to abstaining from resorting to what Horace called *labor limae*, "the slow work of the lime". This tendency could already be traced in the phrase, "to pass to the act". While "passage to the act", envisaged as an event, fortunately leaves unanswered the question of whether an agent intervenes here and who it could be,[16] the formula "to pass to the act" suggests that someone acts and, what's more (as we have seen), does so while knowing what he is doing. If some kind of un-being comes to inhabit the analyst at the end of an analysis, it is not because he has searched for it, let alone wanted it, or desired it.[17] We simply admit that the analyst did not impede what took place – and that is already a lot. The same applies to un-charity. Both, un-being and un-charity, fall within what is called the neutral. A fine illustration of the neutral can be found in Lacan's interpretation of the so-called dream of "Irma's injection".[18]

The promotion of the psychanalytic act, mixed with the passage to the act, is not without a counterpart. One would occupy oneself in rendering this act so marvellously dignified only by associating it with its dark reverse side: the psychoanalyst's "passage to the sexual act".[19] The former is celebrated to the extent that the latter is condemned; the latter is denounced all the more severely as the former is valued. We await the word "transgression" and, indeed, here it comes: "the transgressive sexual passage to the act" (p. 92). Discreet but certainly no less present, morality and its duality of good and evil make a strong and open entry here. What law, then, is being transgressed? As we know, in the West, sexual acts performed by a person is a position of power on someone who, submitting to this power, has accepted that person's advances,[20] are always more severely condemned. Recently (in 2018), a North American university distributed a memorandum that made it clear that a lecturer is obliged to not fool around (it's likely that this term did not appear in this type of memorandum) with anyone taught by him or her. A simple reminder, one may think. Yes, but does this mean that any sleeping around on campus is forbidden from now on, even if the person is not part of the same department as the potential seducer imagined by the administration? Is this the order of social law that one thinks about when denouncing the transgressing psychoanalyst? Very probably. As for knowing whether Lacan was speaking about this same law in order to link it more closely to desire – there is reason to doubt it …

However, this social law is specified here. We read that the psychoanalyst is "the guardian of the setting" (p. 92): as such he/she must "stay on course", and his listening must serve to de-eroticise the analysand (p. 96). There is, we read, "deviation from analytic protocol when the desire of the analyst no longer fulfils its function of being a barrier to jouissance" (p. 93). Guardian, setting, course, barrier, protocol: these are all little soldiers at war[21] against an erotic configuration envisaged as feasible and seen as dramatically as possible. We await the word "trauma" and, sure enough, it appears on p. 93. This kind of discourse is so predictable, so convenient and so conformist with what modern society demands from "health professionals"[22] and, therefore, so conventional, that referring to it here is of no interest other than to allow us to point out the unfortunate indications of "technique" that the discourse conveys, as well as the no less spurious theoretical bases upon which it relies.

A problem of technique: an analyst who adheres to maintaining at all costs "the setting" would be prevented from practising. The reason is that many turning points of an analysis are played out, not within the setting, but in the crossing of the setting's so-called boundaries. Keeping the boundaries fluctuating sometimes has the effect of allowing the analysand to go and seek the analyst there, to interrogate his position in the transference. What we know of the practices of Freud, Ferenczi, Lacan[23] and many others offers many, vivid testimonies of this. I say "so-called" boundaries because, among the transformations of analytic practice that Lacan implemented (apart from the most well-known, the so-called "short" session), there is an absence of any contract between the analyst and the future analysand, which would supposedly, once and for all, define the setting of the analysis. It is quite possible to determine the cost, the number and times of sessions without any kind of initial contract that both the analyst and analysand would sign, and which they would both, from then on, have to respect in all circumstances. A contract goes against the eminently transient and fragile character of initial decisions, which can then be modified without going against a "contract". There are no contracts other than those validated by a lawyer, a civil registrar or, indeed, a gangster.

A problem of theory: what would make the above-mentioned contract useful, valuable and even necessary *for the psychoanalyst*? What would this contract guarantee? First of all, as "guardian of the setting", he would not be able to get out of it himself; however, as guardian, he is located, like a prison guard, both inside and outside. The danger of such an exit – that is, as such, privileged: the passage to the transgressive sexual act – only appears enormous insofar as the analysand and the analyst form a couple: the "analyst-analysand couple" (p. 96). A couple plus a contract ... Here they are then, if not married, at the very least civil partners. Reference is made here to the couple thought of as the "meeting of two desires" (p. 100). Has anyone ever seen such a thing? Has anyone ever seen (on the same page) "two protagonists whose signifying intersection could wreak havoc"?

In summary, this morality starts with the belief in the existence of a sexual relation (clearly indicated by the hyphen in "analyst-analysand couple"). Unburdened by this belief, the analyst can have no need of this morality, which now appears as a defence put up against the inexistence of the sexual relation.

If you have not given in to the inclination to kill yourself after reading all this "Lacanian" drivel, you can return to something serious by taking up once again the thread (glimpsed in the introduction) of the epic leap as it presents itself in jihadist acts, which are all too quickly named "passages to the act". It seems that a jihadist act is, instead, an epic leap (Benslama[24]) and that, just like the passage to the act, this action can only be analysed by being situated in the space [*entre-deux*, also refers to interval] between-two-deaths.[25] It would be wrong to see in what is called "spirituality" an ideality that is detached from the entire dimension of the body or, more precisely, the flesh.[26] We will leave it here without, however, denying that other dimensions are present in jihadism, which are not for me to discuss and which, moreover, I do not have the competence to expound.

West of the Jordan river

Here is a brief but lucid scene from the documentary by Amos Gitaï, *West of the Jordan River*. Amos Gitaï and a child are talking to each other calmly, seated on a bench in Hebron – one of the places where the Israeli-Palestine conflict is at its most tense. We do not really know how old the child is: maybe ten? Or twelve? His first name is Ali, and we learn that he attends school and works well. Their conversation is being mediated by a translator, called Moussa, as Ali does not speak English, the language in which Amos Gitaï is talking to him.

AMOS GITAÏ: Moussa, ask Ali what his dream for Hebron is.
MOUSSA: What is your dream, your wish in life?
ALI (smiling and looking straight at Amos):   My dream is to die as a martyr.
AMOS (who must have understood something of what was said):   Whoa ...
MOUSSA: He's laughing and says that his goal is to be a martyr.
AMOS: Really? He wants to die?
(The question is off the mark and is immediately corrected.)
MOUSSA: He wants to be a martyr, not merely die.
AMOS: Why?
(Someone walks past and Ali greets him politely.)
ALI: Because.
AMOS: But if you die, it's over. It's all over.
MOUSSA (Ali is still smiling):   He says that it's better.
AMOS: But you can only die once.
(This remark ignores the second death.)
ALI: So?
AMOS:(adjusting his question):   What do you hope for after death?
MOUSSA: He says that he will be next to God.
AMOS: What will you say to God?
MOUSSA   (Ali is serious, no longer smiling): He will say I died a martyr.
AMOS: And what does he want God to say to him?
MOUSSA: That he did well.

From what we have heard, can we state that Ali is a terrorist in the making? Already a terrorist? Does he see his life as devoted to spreading terror?

Asking this question allows us to glimpse the response. Those who wage their holy war (jihad) are called "terrorists" only by those who are struck by terror. While they terrorise, they consecrate their lives, their often-murderous actions, their deaths and their eternity to something else, something that we heard Ali say: that God should tell them that they have done well. To terrorise is not, in a decisive manner, what directs their lives.

In 1962, Raymond Aron defined terrorist action as follows: "A violent action is named an act of terrorism when its psychological effects are out of proportion to its purely physical results."[27] Defining an event by its effects is not inappropriate – but remains partial. Today, in France, we remain focused on ourselves each time "terrorist" is uttered in place of "jihadist", which should be chosen if we take into account the spiritual dimension of jihad. Because of fear and a political tendency that excludes spirituality, the Western use of the term "terrorist" neglects the required analysis as soon as we are attacked, injured, killed. To misname the enemy is to jeopardise the knowledge of what has occurred, right up to the awaited result of the combat. This is what happened when France officially spoke not of "war" but of "events" in Algeria.[28] This error in perspective was signalled several times by Fethi Benslama.[29] The root, *j-h-d*, of jihad, means "effort" and refers to the believer on the quest for moral perfection. Moving away from the denomination "terrorist" should not be surprising. One of the experts on this issue, Marc Sageman,[30] said that he did not like this term, which was used by Vichy to designate those who called themselves "resistants" (a name that remains attributed to them: once again, history is the history of those who win). Sageman specifies they are *mujahidin*, soldiers: they are at war, and their war is holy. While including its part of truth, "terrorist" could well be based on the criticism that Edward Said, a Palestine-American writer, addressed to orientalism: its knowledge is constructed; it invents the other and, indeed, ignores and denies it.[31] The same can be said of the term *kamikaze*,[32] aimed at the Japanese.

Things may be changing as far as the term "terrorist" is concerned. We can see an indication of this in the remark by Roger-Pol Droit, quoted in an article in *Le Monde* (13 October 2017), in which he discusses the work, *Djihadisme* by Jacob Rogozinski:[33] "The blindness that prevented the perception of the religious dimension of terrorism has gradually given way to an acknowledgement of it." However, we remain sceptical because, a few lines later, the author persists in seeing in terror and terrorism the very object of future investigations.

Quite recently (5 April 2018), an article in *Libération* reported on a work that argues against the "blindness" of a part of sociology that seeks to explain the "radicalism" of "terrorists" by referring to the discrimination and exclusion to which they are subjected and which lead to their being *radicalised*. This term [in French] has racist connotations. In it, we hear the word "rat" [pronounced in French as /rʌ/], which was commonly used in France during the Algerian war of independence, when the Arabs were seen as "rats", and the brutality of the police and army towards them was called "ratonnade" [often translated in English as "racist attack"]. The work *La Tentation radicale*[34] demonstrates that the most important factor that leads certain people to jihadism is not economic or social but religious. This is confirmed by someone who, having been director of the Mossad for 14 years, is without doubt one who knows this to be the case. On 22 April 2018, *Le Monde* published an interview during which Efraim Halevy (then aged 84) declared that "a very strong religious commitment exists in the Arab world". He went on to say:

> The leaders of Hamas – I hate to admit this – have a better understanding of what is happening in Israel than the contrary, their leaders have stayed for years in our prisons: they have studied us, learned our language. We are victims of our own propaganda in declaring that we do not speak to murderous terrorists. They are also human beings who think.[35]

11 September 2001 – determined to set the West straight

I am not asserting that *all* jihadists have reached the high degree of spirituality demonstrated by the young Ali.[36] Not being a sociologist or an anthropologist, I know nothing of *all* jihadists. On the other hand, I have kept in my archives a page from *Le Monde* (2 October 2002) entitled, "*Le dernier soir avant le 11 Septembre*" ["The last evening before the 11 September"]. Here, too, a particular spirituality is, oh, so present. *Le Monde* obtained permission from the FBI to translate and publish these documents.[37]

Figure 1.1 Copies of documents found in the luggage of Mohammed Atta, the ruins of the Pentagon and in a car abandoned in an airport parking lot.

The FBI did not have to try very hard to find this text. Three copies were found in the places clearly specified above. A kind of signature. Here is the West set straight.

Le Monde describes these four pages as a "collection of religious and practical instructions before the passage to the act", and chooses one extract, which was emphasised by being put within a frame, about "terrifying *the hearts of those who do not believe*". It is the un-believer, *in his heart*, that is targeted, not the citizens of a country, young Western revellers, the politics of a country or whatever else one could put in there, and which would have second place.

The preparatory gestures of the act, which are already part of it, are eminently spiritual: care of the body (shaving, cleansing); blessing of the body – "For this, they read verses in someone's hands, then they rub their hands above the person they wish to bless"; reading of the holy Koran; in the morning, common prayer; purification of the soul; forgetting of the life here below; recalling phrases about the divine will; ablutions just before leaving; supplications during the journey to the airport and once there – "Lord, I ask you for the best of this place and to protect me from its evil"; words to be said, and thus "imposed" but not exactly in the sense that Lacan attributed to them, that is, "God is all that we lack", "there is no other God that God"; recalling that only God deserves to be feared and that this fear is an "immense adoration" (here a valuable light is cast on the symptom called "phobia"); renewed supplications at the moment of boarding the aeroplane, and then in taking the pilots' seats; asking God to grant martyrdom; the cry, "*Allah Akbar*" at the moment of striking; and, even more strange, and all the more incongruous to Western eyes, recalling that "if you kill, *do not cause the one you kill any suffering* [emphasis mine[38]], as this was one of the practices of the prophet"; discarding all will for vengeance, in other words, ensuring that the act will be for God alone. The example given is that of Ali ben Talib, companion and close relative of the prophet Mohammed, who – spat upon by the non-believer with whom he was fighting, did not strike him in return – and waited to kill him when the fight was over, remaining in battle and refusing to react to the insult. Finally, this, quoted in full: "*It is beautiful* [emphasis mine[39]] that someone reads these words of God: 'And those who prefer life after this world must fight for the love of God'." And, furthermore, these words concerning those who seek the jihadist war (incomprehensible if one thinks of "terrorism"), "Do not believe that those who killed for the love of God are dead; they are living …".

Therefore, is not the killing of the body that is in question, but that the hearts, of non-believers, must be attacked even when their hearts stop beating. Thus, we cannot see where to situate those hearts that are eternally blessed, other than in the space between-two-deaths, one side of which may be that of eternal death. Shouldn't we appeal to Muslim theologians to shed light on this issue to frightened spirits?

Nonetheless, it so happens that a such blindness gives way to a few brief moments of possible lucidity. On 26 February 2019, *Le Monde* devoted two pages to the words of Al-Mourbitoune, a jihadist from the Sahel, which were introduced as "a rare and complete testimony". His first commitment to Islam did not owe anything to the jihad. He left "the poor sand of Nouakchott" for the reason that there could be "wine and unhealthy words" there. The attacks of 11 September 2001 made him question God: Did he order that? His commitment followed, summed up in the declaration that he remains the jihadist that he became: "I absolutely do not regret my actions. I did it all for God."

Guillaume Monod devoted a chapter of his book, *En prison, les paroles de djihadistes*,[40] to the theological thinking that ISIS has made its own, which is focused on defilement and its opposite, purity. A prison psychiatrist, Monod spoke with many jihadists, some of whom wanted to see him regularly and for several months. He restores the honour of his profession, which has been mishandled – as we have seen – by some of his colleagues. Refusing to go down the common slope that maintains that the "terrorist" has nothing at all in common with anyone in the West, he endeavours, on the contrary and as often as possible, to break this segregation, thus rendering their humanity to the jihadists – without, however, legitimising their murderous actions. As a psychiatrist, he ceaselessly discards the references that his profession could provide, which he considers inappropriate. Perversity does not explain the passage to the act (p. 95); to embrace death is not based on a pleasure in killing, nor is it a feature of an "uncultivated barbarian who loves death simply for the sake of perverse excitement" (pp. 134–135); "Desensitisation to death is not the symptom of perverse functioning" (p. 146); and "Fascination with violence is not necessarily a pathological manifestation" (p. 139).

Having avoided the trap that psychiatric knowledge, among others, held out to him, Monod gave himself the freedom to use other references. These make the jihadist the neighbour, albeit not a close one, of each of us. Has Christianity never engaged in a spiritual crusade, even today (p. 29)? To wish to be part of a community of believers, and even inhabit a city of God on Earth, is that so strange (pp. 31–32)? While acknowledging the "fundamentalist" nature of such a community, Monod likens it to American fundamentalism, born at the same time (p. 87). He notes that not wanting to differentiate the moral, the religious, the legal and the political, echoes the positions maintained (successfully, we know) by Billy Graham and Jerry Falwell (p. 123) and recalls the adoption of *In God We Trust* as the official motto of the United States in 1956 (p. 88). With regard to the promise, made to whoever dies a martyr, that he will find in paradise 70 (or 72) virgins, Monod abstains from the facile explanation of this as "the sexual fantasy of an immature adolescent" (p. 137). He observes that this is the "promise of a pure sexuality", in the same way that the use of the veil brings to the sexual act (p. 111).

"I know what I am doing" and "I scorn the dust of which I am made and that speaks to you": these words of Saint Just (quoted on p. 91) are the same as those of the jihadist, who Monod also likens to Antigone, the "figure who best incarnates what's at stake in jihadism" (p. 106) as she relinquishes nothing of divine law. Such knowledge, as we have said, incites us to situate the jihadist act, not as a passage to the act, but as an epic leap. The terms "epic" and "saga" appear several times in these pages by Monod who, therefore, crosses paths with the clinical discovery of Benslama, although he clearly disagrees with the latter as far as so-called "de-radicalisation" is concerned (p. 163). While the support of Plotinus taken on by the theological thinking of ISIS is mentioned (p. 70), other more recent references are also telling. He thus observes that the description of the "initiatory" journey of those who went to join the fight of ISIS against Bashar el-Assad in Syria can be found in sagas as well-known as *Star Wars*, *The Lord of the Rings* or *Harry Potter* (p. 103). One can also refer to Philip Roth's *American Pastoral*, when Seymour Levov's daughter, who set off bombs and killed four people, dives head-first into Jainism, (in Sanskrit, *jina* means "victorious"). The core narrative of the story is the same as that that rules jihadist commitment. Once a jihadist arrives in Syria, a new name is given to him, as is still the case today when a Christian enters a monastic order. Rather than seeing in this the manifestation of some phenomenon of a psychopathological order, Monod recalls (p. 110) that it was the same with Abram (contraction of *Abou Ram*, the most high father) when God wanted to seal his alliance with him: he would thereafter be called Abraham (*Abou Raham*, father of the multitude, father of nations).

Having re-given the jihadist[41] his humanity ("re-given", certainly not from the jihadist's point of view as he never lost it), as we have just established, Monod then concludes his work (p. 160) with a quotation of George Steiner. The least that one can say about it is that it poses a question that no one can evade: a common question then, even though the responses or absences thereof are diverse:

> To have neither heaven nor hell is to find oneself intolerably deprived of everything, in a world that is absolutely flat. Of the two, hell has appeared as the easier one to reconstitute. We must admit that the descriptions of hell have always been far more detailed. In our present barbarism (the point was made after the Shoah), there is at work a defunct theology, a collection of references to transcendence which, in their slow death, have given way to parodic forms, to substitutes. The end of belief, the passage of religious faith to hollow convention is being revealed as a more dangerous process than the philosophers foresaw.[42]

Here, once again, we "meet" Lacan, for whom "desire is hell". Which hell? Certainly not that in which one burns eternally while crying for a heavenly jouissance that has definitely been lost. More appropriate to what Lacan could have had in mind, is that other hell, the hell of Angelus Silesius a "living in hell without hell",[43] as the same apophatic approach characterises the link of the Silesian to hell and that of the subject to the non-existent Other. Or, at a more trivial level, could it be the hell of libraries? Another hell, no doubt, situated between two hells.

Notes

1 The introduction to Michel Angot's book, *Les Mythes des Indes* (Paris, Éditions du Seuil, 2019) offers a much wider perspective on the problem rapidly outlined above.
2 Much depends on the "somehow", which few readers of *Le Monde* would notice, while others would await more precision.
3 Cf. Ines Rieder, Diana Voigt, *Sidonie Csillag, Homosexuelle chez Freud, lesbienne dans le siècle*, translated from German by Thomas Gindele (Paris, Epel, 2003). At the time of the publication of this work, it was decided to not make Magarethe Csonka's name public.
4 In Sigmund Freud, *La Technique psychanalytique*, translated from German by Anne Berman (Paris, Puf, 1953, republished 2002, p. 108) (underlining by Freud).
5 Seminar, *L'Angoisse*, session of 23 January 1963, during which Lacan enhanced "monstration" with a term of his own, "montrage".
6 I discuss this point in *Ombre de son chien, Discours psychanalytique, discours lesbian* (Paris, Epel, 2004).
7 *La Clinique lacanienne*, no. 23, Toulouse, Érès. As well as its director and sub-editor, the review is composed of an editorial editing committee for France, a reading committee and a scientific committee, all of which making up around 60 people (of several nationalities). One may thus deduce that *La Clinique lacanienne* is representative of what one could call the current state of Jacques Lacan's presence in people's (although not everyone's) minds. For this reason, I believed that it was not possible to neglect this edition devoted to the passage to the act.
8 The term analysand in Lacan implied an active subject ($), not a passive patient. (Ed. note.)
9 This author did not hesitate to refer to "a good old neurotic from the good old days", with whom it was "very pleasant to work" (p. 84). Another contributor had no hesitation in stating that (p. 105), on reaching the passage to the act, "the subject nonetheless remained caught up in the meanderings of sadomasochism". Is it possible to give any credit to this statement when what is in question in the same text is "homosexual flirting in all its sad reality"?
10 We read: "It's the psychoanalytic definition of 'the passage to the act' that consists of 'acting without remembering', as Freud wrote." The author must have had some suspicion of writing something stupid as he put *passage to the act* in inverted commas. And, indeed, Freud never wrote this. You would search in vain to find in his work any mention of the notion of "passage to the act". His *agieren*, as opposed to "working-through", has – countless times – been acknowledged as being "acting-out". (As we shall see, this error is also shared by those beyond Lacanian circles.)
11 Here, without any substantiation, the idea that it is the fantasm that passes to the act is stated – which, in Lacan, would not make any sense.
12 In the same contribution, we read (p. 40) that "the sexual relation includes a hole", whereas what Lacan said and repeated a hundred times is that what made a hole was the impossibility – recognised by him – of writing the sexual relation.
13 *L'Ordinaire du psychanalyste* was, at the time, the title selected for a review put together by some of those who opposed Lacan's dissolution of L'École freudienne de Paris, who moreover went as far as resorting to the law trying to stop the dissolution of L'École in order to make it exist just as history had made it come about, no doubt for eternity.
14 The dignity of the psychoanalyst is written about several times by this contributor (p. 9, p. 101 and p. 105). The contrast between this self-proclaimed dignity and the *dignus est intrare*, which, Lacan says, is announced by the accreditation panel when they name a *passant* [the person passing] as "Analyst of the School". This recognition is not even direct: it dispenses with the face-to-face meeting of the panel

and the candidate; it takes the path of the testimony of the *passeurs* [those who pass the testimony of the candidate] (Jacques Lacan, session 14 October 1972, L'École belge de la psychanalyse, available at *Pas-tout Lacan*, https://ecole-lacanienne.net).
15 In the conclusion of *L'Autresexe* (Paris, Epel, 2015), I presented some incarnations of what this "*déchariter*" could be.
16 See below, Chapters II and III.
17 In view of the self-promotion that followed, we come to regret that Lacan put forward a "desire of the psychoanalyst".
18 I discussed this interpretation in *Lettre pour lettre. Transcrire, traduire, translittérer* (Toulouse, Érès, 1984, pp. 253–254), emphasising its point by means of an aphorism of Lichtenberg: "That one dreams so many mad things does not surprise me; what surprises me is that one believes that one is the person who does and thinks all these things."
19 Would asexual passages to the act then exist?
20 Do we wish to remove the erotic from all relation to power (power of money, prestige, beauty, social status, sex, etc.)? There would have to be a lot of other regulations.
21 On p. 92, the author evokes "enemies of the cure".
22 Are they not, rather, sickness professionals?
23 With regard to Lacan, please refer to my work, Jean Allouch, *Les impromptus de Lacan. 543 bons mots recueillis par Jean Allouch* (Paris, Mille et une Nuits, 2009).
24 Fethi Benslama is a Tunisian psychoanalyst. For more information, see https://fr.wikipedia.org/wiki/Fethi_Benslama.
25 I recently put forward a discussion of this in Chapter II of *La Scène lacanienne et son cercle magique. Des fous se soulèvent* (Paris, Epel, 2017).
26 Should we recall the blood of Christ; the Christian mystic becoming waste; the bodies thrown from Aztec pyramids; the Buddhist monk refusing desire; the Hindu drinking the milk of Shiva in the temple; etc.?
27 Raymond Aron, *Paix et guerre entre nations* (Paris, Calman-Lévy, 1962, p. 176). I owe this reference to a passage in the work of Guillaume Monod, mentioned later.
28 The term, "Algerian war", was officially adopted by France on 18 October 1999, 27 years after the end of hostilities.
29 Fethi Benslama, *Un furieux désir de sacrifice, le surmusulman* (Paris, Éditions du Seuil, 2016). Myram Benraad observed that the militarisation of "jihad" is in part due to European orientalism, then taken up by politico-religious integrationism at the beginning of the twentieth century. Jihads fought against the Soviets in Afghanistan. This conflict was the origin of the 1998 proclamation of "global jihad" by Bin Laden (Myriam Benraad, *Jihad: des origins religieuses à l'idéologie*, Paris, Le Cavalier bleu, 2017, and *Libération*, 1 February 2018).
30 Heard on France Culture (*La matinale*), 10 November 2017.
31 Edward Said, *L'Orientalisme créé par l'Occident* (Paris, Éditions du Seuil, 1980). Also, Victor Hugo, in "Lui" ["Him"], a poem about Napoleon's glory: "Sublime, il apparut aux tribus éblouies / Tel un Mahomet d'Occident" [Sublime, he appeared to the awe-struck tribes / Like a Mohammed of the East"].
32 The literal meaning of *kamikaze* is: "divine wind" and originated in Japan's thirteenth century when the Mongol invasion fleet under Kublai Khan was destroyed by a typhoon. (Ed. note.)
33 Jacob Rogozinski, *Djihadisme: le retour du sacrifice* (Paris, Desclée De Brouwer, 2017).
34 Anne Muxel and Olivier Galland, *La Tentation radicale* (Paris, Puf, 2018).
35 There is an echo here of the letter that Freud addressed to Keren HaYesod on 26 February 1930, in which he wrote: "The unrealistic fanaticism of our co-believers has some responsibility in the rise of Arab defiance" (quoted in Eran Rolnik, *Freud à Jérusalem. Psychanalyse face au sionisme*, essay, preface by Abraham B. Yehoshua, translated from Hebrew by Gilles Rozier, Paris, L'Antilope, 2017).

36 One may object that, far from proving anything at all, Ali was manipulated, influenced by a militant entourage, the Qatari television channel Al Jazeera or even video games. The words he spoke would, therefore, not be his own. This objection does not hold up because, in being able to be referred to what it is stating, it self-destructs.
37 It is a translation (into French) of a translation from Arabic into English.
38 In *Les Bienvienveillantes*, Jonathan Littell reports that those who took pleasure in inflicting pain or in killing were eliminated from the SS (Paris, Le Grand Livre du Mois, 2006).
39 Please refer to the function of the beautiful as presented by Lacan in his seminar, *L'Éthique de la psychanalyse* (see *Pas-tout Lacan,* https://ecole-lacanienne.net).
40 Guillame Monod, *En prison, les paroles de djihadistes* (Paris, Gallimard, 2018).
41 "Human" is not opposed here to "inhuman" but includes it – which should be the case.
42 George Steiner, *Dans le château de Barbe-Bleue* (Paris, Gallimard, coll. "Folio essais", 2008, p. 67).
43 *Le Pèlerin chérubinique*, distique I, 39 (quoted by Jacques le Brun), *Dieu un pur rien. Angelus Silesius. Poésie, métaphysique et mystique* (Paris, Éd du Seuil, 2019, p. 166).

Chapter II

To think, to act: Louis Althusser

> But when I speak of wanting to do something, it's not like wanting to go to the theatre. If you are sleepy, it's not that you want to sleep ... you go to sleep.
> [...]
> It's the same. I didn't want to kill: it so happened that something natural just followed [...] something that comes and which you don't control.
>
> Ricardo Melogno[1]

In March 2018, a theatrical version of *L'Avenir dure longtemps*[2] ("The future lasts a long time"), was shown in Paris. The fact that I went to see it would be of no other interest here – apart from extracts of the text itself, so judiciously selected – if it were not for Michel Bernard's mise-en-scène and Angelo Bison's performance, both of which allow us to clearly perceive a feature that could be missed in only reading the work.

It was a manner of presentation that had a bearing on a very particular exploitation of the theatrical space: one was aware of it even when it was not realised physically.[3] Situated as a witness in relation to the character of Althusser, face-to-face with him (in an interpellation), the audience becomes part of the play. Here he is, this fellow man: the audience is transported onto the stage. From then on, and as soon as they are there, where can they report their testimony? The auditorium itself is empty – the place that should be occupied by another, very different audience: the one that Louis Althusser despaired about ever being able to address, the one that could legitimately make a pronouncement about the murderous act that left everyone speechless, starting with Louis Althusser himself, at least initially [*dans un premier temps*].[4] The theatrical performance makes noticeable this absence. Nothing will ever come to fill the hole that a metonymy indicates: the judgement that has not taken place.

DOI: 10.4324/9781003504092-3

Taken as witness, "brought in": what is the audience invited to report in this place, a place where there is definitely no one to receive their report? These witnesses are also asked to resonate somewhere other than within themselves the title sentence: "The future lasts a long time" (*L'Avenir dure longtemps*). And so, through the effect of this particular device, in keeping with the enunciative situation in which Althusser found himself through and after the murder, the theatre allows this sentence to be heard. It is not so much a statement, but as a cry, the cry of one who has *disappeared*. Whoever does not die, but disappears, is condemned to a future that lasts for *too long* a time. It never stops lasting, this future – the lasting is not time, which sometimes passes without leaving any time. There is no *kairos* in the lasting, no event. Lasting takes away something eminently precious: that is, what one can trivially call "dying". The intolerable hardness of lasting (*Intolérable dureté du durer*).

Allow me now to recount a childhood memory. It was in 1944, and I was five years old. Military authorities had told a young neighbour that her fiancé, a soldier of our defeated army, had been reported missing. I was able to observe her *during* the years [*des années* durant], wondering every time she crossed a road whether he was going to reappear from the left or the right. She never recovered from this, Marina Coste. She never believed or knew if her beloved was dead ... A different kind of eternal fiancée to the one Kierkegaard wanted.

This kind of "immortality" is not the kind that celebrity offers to a few chosen ones – for a moment at least, because these celebrities end up disappearing even from the Web and thus meet what awaits everyone: not just physical death, but the second death after which no trace remains of the person who once lived, and in which there remains no memory in anyone's mind of the person. Hinduism is aware of the sort of peace that the second death offers to everyone. The belief according to which after death, everyone is reincarnated – again and again, forever – is horrifying. Hinduism has a name, *moksha*, to designate the liberating second death that puts an end to successive and indefinite reincarnations. The Bible itself does not overlook the second death: "Blessed and holy are those who share in the first resurrection. The second death has no power over them."[5] This future that lasts forever, this eternity, deprives the subject of his second death. After the murder followed by no prosecution, Althusser, the one who disappeared, knew that he was condemned to never die. One who disappears does not die: Is there any worse condemnation?[6]

Because of this, two pages by Jean-Claude Milner, recently devoted to Althusser,[7] are clarified. Milner here discusses the successive "confinements": the Stalag, la rue d'Ulm, illness, crime.[8] Milner writes that Althusser "marked out his life" with these confinements; and, furthermore, that confinement "allowed him to escape the curses of the Bystander" – as if he were responsible for this. Here, Althusser is not taken as a subject but rather as an agent of these confinements. (Since Lacan and, now, after the works of Alain de Libera, we can no longer disregard this distinction.[9]) In order to escape the Bystander, Althusser would have, in some way, wanted these confinements, which were instigated and put in place. Only the "crime" in Milner's list is retained by us, but discarding any affirmation that Althusser was its agent. If there is a confinement – of which there is no doubt – it can be situated only in what followed the murder, which the murder *at once* put in place (we will come to this): that is, his status as one who has disappeared.

The farewell letter written by a *normalien* (student of *L'École Normale Supérieure*) to his former professor is from someone who has not acknowledged the radical rejection of psychology, so clear-cut in André Gide and Georges Canguilhem, and then extended by many others, including Michel Foucault and Jacques Lacan. By making the subject an agent – and not, as in Lacan, a *pure supposed* –, psychology burdens the subject with a responsibility that is, properly speaking, undue. Nonetheless, it is possible to consider differently what happened, and what has remained in suspense: a suspense in which there is no guarantee that, one day, its interminable being could end. The rest of this text is going to be applied to taking this into account, in an attempt to clarify, with regard to Althusser, the interplay between thinking and the act, as this is manifested in the passage to the act and its surrounds.

The beneficial effects of psychoanalysis have been so strongly attributed to "speaking", to "the interpretation", to "the symbolic", that it seems useful (without, however, excluding the above effects) to present a certain version, *in vivo*, of Jacques Lacan's practice that plays a different chord – that of the act. As it was attested by the rumours spreading Lacan's impromptu quips among the members of *L'École freudienne*, that I compiled and published,[10] I will rescue only one of them, entitled "To dream matters" (*Rêver compte*):

The analysand: I dreamed that ...

Lacan, *interrupting him*: That's good. See you tomorrow.

Being outraged by this very brief and no doubt expensive session, would be to neglect the transferential situation, which one may nonetheless imagine, and which justifies this cutting-off and brevity. The analysand was not prevented from speaking: quite the contrary. He had been showering the analyst with his dreams, supposing that this is what the analyst expected from him, "This is what you want, so here it is!". Preventing him, in an almost physical way, from going on, amounts to giving him an understanding that, far from speaking, he was drowning the fish (in this case, the analyst); that the analyst was not especially fond of his dreams; and that he was not allowing himself to be taken in by this demand that was acted upon a supposedly Freudian complicity.[11] The analysand was enacting this transference and only an act could both take it into account and offer him the possibility of configuring himself differently. This is, moreover, what happened as the analysand, *delighted*, immediately rushed to laughingly recount his memorable session to his friends.

One would be mistaken to think that this kind of transferential shift could be accessible to interpretation: insofar as the interpretation was the problem here, it could not provide the solution.

We will return to the root of this problem if we admit, with Lacan, that – on the one hand – the subject in analysis is the same Cartesian subject seeking, not so much knowledge, as certainty and – on the other hand – he differs from this because what Descartes was aiming for was to "see clearly in [his] actions"[12] (discourse of a master) whereas in analysis, as in life, thought can both guide and mislead action. Furthermore, the rule of free association breaks that kind of false authority that someone confers upon himself by preceding a statement with the words, "I think that ..." or "It is true that ..." (like Gottlob Frege).

Act or interpretation (more generally, thought): we will retain the distinction between these two registers in order to interrogate not only Althusser's murderous act but also, closely tied to it, the absence of the act that followed, noted previously as having taken place at once. In this regard, Hegel provides a precise statement: an event is not judged in itself, but by its results. Such, then, is the event that was the murder of Hélène on 16 November 1980. I do not say "of his wife" because to say this would mean closing the question of who was killed or, rather, the question of what was put to an end. Here, "Hélène" has no other value than being tied to Althusser's cry, "I have strangled Hélène!". After this event, there was the non-act of judgement – non-act ... we will soon be led to revisit this problem from Althusser's point of view. The murder did not rebound in another act, but ran aground, in the sense that a ship runs aground – not in the sense that, according to Lacan, the characteristic of any act is to be missed (*d'étre manqué*) [*parapraxis*].

It is appropriate to refer again to this in order to clarify the interplay in Althusser between the action and the absence of the act that followed.

Thus, then, we have the formula, "either I do not think, or I am not", that Lacan extracted from Descartes' "I think therefore I am", by extending and dismembering it – to the point of forging an alternative: a so-called "*alienating vel*", qualified as at once "necessary", "forced" and "inevitable", demanding that only one or another branch of the alternative be chosen.[13]

The *vel* was first mentioned during a conference that Lacan gave at the Sorbonne, on 9 May 1957.[14] Here, he found himself "blindsided for a moment by [his] audience" for having stated: "I think where I am not, therefore I am where I do not think."[15] Nonetheless, this statement was not questioned just after that day but, instead, ten years later.[16] This period of delay (from 9 May 1957 to 11 January 1967[17]) could have been longer if it was acknowledged that Lacan had read the manuscript of an article that he co-signed in 1936 with Alexandre Kojève, entitled "*Hegel et Freud. Essai d'une confrontation interpretative*".[18] The Cartesian fact, Kojève put forward, "is necessarily double ... both a revealed-Being and a revealing-Being: it is as much Being as thought (of the Being revealing the being)" (p. 204). Not 10, then, but

30 years of latency. The midpoint (27 June 1962) is to be marked with a white [*blanche*] stone or, even better, by a "*blanchote*" stone (play on words: see below, Maurice Blanchot stone). On that day, Lacan spoke in his seminar of *Thomas l'Obscur*. He recognised in Blanchot someone who, with "The Stopping of Death" (*L'Arrêt de mort*), offered him "the confirmation of what [he] had said about the second death all year in the seminar on ethics.[19] Nothing is said, however, of a page in this work where Blanchot makes his reader aware of "these sweet words: 'I think, therefore I am not'."[20]

We have hardly strayed away from Althusser with these two references: one to the second death, and the other to the dislocation of what the *cogito* had linked: thinking and being.[21] We will move even closer to him by recalling that Lacan made "I do not think" a major characteristic of the passage to the act. We may as well say, following the unfolding of the *cogito*, that it is a matter of his being in the act where the subject finds himself without thought.

Let us recall that we have distinguished two modalities of the act without, for all that, excluding others. Different to the passage to the act, the epic leap is the realisation of a thought as such, articulated and conscious of itself. It makes sense at once; it is inscribed in a history. These two modalities of the act (the passage to the act, the epic leap) can easily be placed in the alternative configured by the *vel* of alienation: *where I think, I am not* (epic leap); *where I am, I do not think* (passage to the act). With Michel Foucault, I give the name "uprising" to the point of departure of the inaugural choice that will select one or the other branch of the alternative, and which it cannot evade. We will return to this point at the conclusion of these pages.

Committed without thinking and even without thoughts, even if unconscious, the murder of Hélène presents many characteristics of the passage to the act. We can relate to this action a statement made about Claire Lannes, the protagonist of *L'Amante anglaise*: "It could be that a minute before killing her, she didn't think that she was going to kill her"[22] (see Chapter III). The apparent continuity of the action veering from massage (Althusser was doing this, it is thought[23]) to strangulation (without thought) hides an abyss, a gap above which nothing passes from one side to the other, from thought acted to the act without thoughts, and it is here that there is "passage to the act". A name, then, that is inappropriate because what happened then – the murder – is in no way a potentially symbolic enunciation that could be realised (*passed to the act*) only inadvertently and for a thousand reasons that one would be hard put to specify. In its 6 May 1992 publication, *Le Canard enchaîné* entitled an article, "*Massage à l'acte*": a nice formula in terms of language but inopportune if one understands the passage to the act as a simple and conclusive intensification of the act of massage.

It's the same with the passage to the act of the Papin sisters. The fact that it gave rise to so many commentaries and artistic creations without any of these productions ever being universally established, indicates an inadequacy, indeed an impossibility of (psychiatric, psychoanalytic, literary, artistic and common) thinking. It, too, is unforeseeable, emerging from no one knows where ... It also runs aground in the way that we have specified, Christine Papin, having resolutely refused to ask for presidential pardon, as she was asked to, let herself die from cachexia without anyone being able to prevent her from doing so.[24] Ten years after his murderous action, and placed in a retirement home in 1990, Althusser also refused to eat or drink. He died not long afterwards (22 October) in La Verrière Clinic, a psychiatric teaching hospital.

While failure goes with bouncing back, things are quite different with running aground, which can be seen as what follows of the passage to the act: its non-conclusive outcome. If every running aground or stranding (like that of a ship at sea) is a failure, every failure is not a running aground. As we have said, disappearing is not an ending, nor a termination: rather, a non-ending. "After the haulers were nailed the coloured posts, the drunken ship, now directionless, remains thus, like a kneeling woman":

> *Glaciers, soleils d'argent, flots nacreux, cieux de braises!*
> *Échouages hideux au fond des golfes bruns*
> *Où les serpents géants dévorés des punaises*
> *Choient, des arbres tordus, avec de noirs parfums!*[25]

Is poetry susceptible to thinking the act without thoughts? Or should we rather conclude that when death has been at work, only a certain silence can respond accurately, albeit badly, to this running aground that calls for no follow-up or response? That any discourse in this regard is merely futile chatter? The situation we face with the passage to the act is the same as we face with mourning: Both of these expel the symbolic in its entirety. There is nothing more awkward, more tenuous and more futile than the condolences offered after a funeral to the deceased's family. They are resounding inanities that both mask and unveil "the inadequacy of all signifying elements to face the hole created in existence by the implementation of the signifying system around the least mourning".[26] Louis Althusser – from the ever non-locatable place where, having disappeared, he resides – would not find this invitation to silence out of context: this invitation to silence that banishes any discourse addressed to him. This is what he himself stated, although in problematic terms: "What can they add to what I write? A commentary? But that's what I'm doing myself!"[27] "Problematic" because it remains utterly clear that the publication of *L'avenir dure longtemps* will not achieve the desired effect – quite the contrary. Louis Althusser formulated this desired effect as follows:

> Now that I am entrusting this very personal book to the public who would like to read it, it is still through this paradoxical bias: *in order to enter definitively into anonymity*, not by the tombstone of the non-place, but in the publication of everything that can be known of me, which will thus forever allow me to be at peace with demands of indiscretion.[28]

Feeding a rumour in order to silence it is wishful thinking: it's a futile endeavour. There will be gossip; it will never stop. It partly turns away from the event and, therefore, betrays it. One may as well admit that what is developing here has the status of false speaking: not in the sense of the true/false binomial, but in the sense of a musician playing out of tune.

This off-kilter speaking, this speaking with no possibility of claiming to be correct, this inadvertent speech with regard to the particular silence evoked by the passage to the act, exceeds an even more radical silence than the one imposed by death. This is because, as we have said, to disappear is not to die (which Althusser knew so well!) but offers the subject a time where he stays in the space [interval] between-two-deaths that offers him no anonymity. Contrary to dying, disappearing deprives the subject of his second death, leaving him to inhabit (confined, Milner would say) the space where, in effect, the future lasts a very long time – indeed, indefinitely.

The above quotation is testament to this: this off-kilter speaking is also Althusser's because we have received certain messages from him (him, who?), even though he is one who has disappeared. We cannot pretend that these words had not been written. What is this about? What can these words make known in, and of, the situation described above? What do they hope to obtain? And from whom?

One may be astonished that the problem should be considered in this way. Someone who has disappeared does not write;[29] just one word from him and he is no longer someone who has disappeared. Nonetheless, even though he tried to do so, Althusser provided the reason – according to him – for this, just after describing his version of the murder scene in *L'Avenir dure longtemps*. Someone spoke "in his place", he noted (which is doubtful); he thought it important to intervene "*personally and publicly* in order to make [his] own testimony heard".[30] He proposed not to just let things be: neither the situation as it was nor, more broadly, his being condemned "to live to the end of [his] days" – and, I would add, well beyond the end of his days: the end of his first death. The last lines of the Foreword are remarkably clairvoyant. He wrote: "It is my lot to believe I can address a concern only by indefinitely incurring others." Writing, therefore, does not provide any effective peace. It's a matter of not disregarding rumours and not allowing them to spread: a matter of countering their development by intervening *in their place* (by putting there instead, as we have read, a "myself") not *from his place* but *since* ("*depuis*" meaning both "from" and "since") *his place*.

No one can control any of the rumours, "it-is-said" ["*on-dit*"] about one's life; no one can know the whole story. As we know, Marguerite Duras highlighted what the "it-is-said" carries from a truth that is inaccessible by any other means. To try to control this "it-is-said", to want to master it, is to discard the truth that is the Neutral (Roland Barthes[31]), the truth of Beckett's "Who cares who speaks?": the truth that Lacan recognised as being the very origin of psychoanalysis. According to Lacan, Freud was so possessed by his dream "of Irma's injection" that his culpability with regard to Irma's persistent illness faded. The voice that relieved him of all responsibility is therefore:

> ... that august Voice
> Which, when it sounds, makes itself known
> As no longer being the voice of anyone.
> Like the voices of waves and forests.[32]

To intervene in place of this rumour, this Neutral, this *it-is-said* ... to intervene in the place of this voice is a negating disquiet. However, nothing is really resolved. The point of the Neutral is not reached by Althusser's writings after Hélène's murder, *and here we are endeavouring nothing other than to indicate that only the passage to the act can reach this point: that it alone has the capacity to reach it.*

The effect of the words written after the act would consist of one concern giving way to several. Must we conclude from this transformation that Althusser – as a writer, having written – is no longer one who has disappeared and the question as it has been presented so far, makes no sense?

We would have to do so if it were not for a certain displacement, even a sleight of hand, made possible by the writing, and then the *post mortem* publication, of *L'Avenir dure longtemps*, which repeats the disquiet. Althusser attributed being placed under "the tombstone of silence" to the "destiny of having no place": something that we cannot endorse, purely and simply. It is the passage to the act that definitively established his status as someone who has disappeared, while "having no place" merely sealed this state. Between two lines written by him, here is the gulf in which he disappeared:

> Il est en train de masser le cou d'Hélène, couchée sur le dos.
>
> Le visage d'Hélène est immobile et serein, ses yeux ouverts fixent le plafond.
>
> ...
>
> Et soudain, je suis frappé de terreur: ses yeux sont interminablement fixes et surtout voici qu'un bref bout de langue repose, insolite et paisible, entre ses dents et ses lèvres.[33]

He is massaging Hélène's neck as she lies on her back.

Her face is still and serene, her open eyes staring at the ceiling.

...

And suddenly, I am stricken with terror. Her eyes are forever fixed and, above all, a tiny bit of her tongue rests, strangely and peacefully, between her teeth and lips.

Hélène serene ... and then peaceful: here is a strange gap, as if nothing had happened – almost. Althusser has never seen the face of someone who had been strangled and yet he writes, he "knew she had been strangled. But how?" The word "how" carries two meanings: "How does he know?" or "How has she been strangled?" In a panic, he shouts, "I have strangled Hélène!". Yes, he knows this: but *not by remembering it*, only from seeing her face and deducing that the act had occurred. The act of murder itself has left no trace. His knowing (afterwards) comes from his having seen: an inference, somehow, in view of the result. While this result showed him, in Hélène, a strangled woman, there was nothing to assure him – apart from this observation after the fact – that there had ever been a strangler.

People have wanted to see this kind of passage to the act in certain violent, often murderous, actions that – when they occurred – were significant enough to interest everyone. This was the case, for example, with Ernst Wagner: he killed several people in the town where he worked as a teacher because of the rumour that he was a homosexual.[34] Because he knew what motivated his act, should we not call it an "epic leap"? Wagner thought about and reflected on his act. Serious in his madness, he first killed his wife and children so that they would not have to be burdened throughout their lives by having a husband and father who was a killer. Should we also recognise an epic leap in the action of Iris Cabezudo, who killed her father, who she believed (truly, in part) never stopped abusing his wife – only to realise, not long after the murder and the dismissal of the case, that it was not so much her father's violence but her mother's incessant complaints that drove her to it.[35]

We are accustomed to seeing the degree of violence in an action as the criterion that distinguishes the passage to the act from other ways of acting (parapraxis, symptomatic act, acting-out, etc.). The clinical discovery of the epic leap compels us to come up with another criterion and to re-view the former: not the violence, but the inscription or lack thereof in a history that immediately makes sense.

When Althusser's action occurred, he knew neither what was happening nor whether he was the agent of what happened. And, moreover, was he the agent? Wouldn't it be more advisable to attribute this syncope to what Marx, following Saint-Simon, called "the power of things" (another name for the Neutral)?

Althusser was not present in his act. He was not there in the sense that he was not even able to say, "I am not". From this, it follows that he was never there, a situation that continues today and finds itself as forever lasting. In this consists the first and foremost point of his disappearance, of his confinement as someone who has disappeared.

Althusser provided another indication about the murder, which can be read in a passage of the manuscript of *L'Avenir dure longtemps*. It consists of two sentences that were not published by the editors of the book, no doubt because they were crossed out by the author: this only serves to show their importance, if it is true that the signifier is the effacement of the trace.[36]

Il n'est pas d'Hallucination du sésir [corrigé désir] de présence sans volonté de détruire la présence[36] qui nie le désir de mort. Cette volonté de destruction peut conduire à la destruction effective de la présence hallucinée, en l'espèce la personne/même[37] qui sert du support à cette presence hallucinée.

There is no hallucination of *sésir* [corrected to desire] for the presence without wanting to destroy the presence[37] that denies the desire for death. This willingness to destroy can lead to the effective destruction of the hallucinated presence, in this case the same/[38] person who serves as a support for the hallucinated presence.

Reading this, can we even qualify as murder, this action aimed at getting rid of a particular presence? Which presence? We are not at all obliged to accord one and the same meaning to the term "presence" in these sentences. Rather, the play on *sésir/désir*, in itself a kind of redoubling, invites us to a closer look. We then distinguish two different presences: the presence that is desired, a kind of pure presence that must be seized, albeit in a hallucinatory way; and the other presence that denies the desire for death and whose destruction alone would provide access to the other. This is feasible because the second presence constitutes the support for the first. Hélène Rytman paid for this with her life, due to an immense misunderstanding.

In 1982, referring again to his act, Althusser wrote the following lines, which clarify what he meant by "support":

> I strangled my wife during an intense and unforeseeable crisis of mental confusion, in November 1980: my wife who was the world to me, who loved me to the point of wanting only to die because she could not live and, no doubt, I – in my confusion and unawareness – did her "this favour", against which she did not defend herself but from which she died.[39]

This support was a *figure*, the figure of someone, "Hélène", who – not being able to live – could only love by wanting to die; or, at least, that is what he thought as it seems unintentional, to say the least, to reduce Hélène to this single characteristic, even supposing that she let herself be isolated. Is there a presence there? Not exactly: what is at play here is only a possible support for a presence that was desired and that only the passage to the act was able to invoke. This passage to the act consists of one word, "Come!". A call, therefore, to a presence: more precisely, to a presence that has been recognised as double following the indication of the term "support". Presence of her, "Hélène", who is all the more intensely awaited in that her desire to die renders her absent to herself and to life. At least, this is how Althusser understood it.[40]

However, another presence intervenes here: another "Come!" which is spoken during the sexual act when the partner is late in "coming": a future that often lasts a long time. One may as well admit that, during the love-making, this partner was, strangely, not acknowledged as present, despite all the caresses and other erotic foreplay – that only coming made her a partner as such, as long as this presence only appears like an evanescent lightning bolt.

"Support" signals the double presence at play in the passage to the act which, failing to reach this double presence, can only aim at making it disappear – and this is only possible by disappearing. We will later, in Chapter III and the Conclusion, rectify these statements as we find ourselves capable of assigning the presence of the hallucinated Hélène to the first analytic of sex (that of the object *a*), and of assigning to the second analytic of sex (that of the inexistent sexual relation), the other presence: the one that, if it were effective, would allow the "seizing" [*sésir*] of the sexual relation.[41] In one case a hallucinated "Hélène", the other case a woman with whom the sexual relation could be written.

When we come to examine the murder committed by Claire Lannes (Chapter III), we will see, as we have here – but in a manner more accessible to analysis – the interplay of these two analytics and to see the passage to the act inscribed in the first analytic of sex, and the epic leap inscribed in the second. In conclusion, we will find this same interplay as we endeavour to clarify what Lacan meant by "enlightened passage to the act", a syntagm that initially appears as teratological but which he nonetheless used in order to question the end of an analysis and the passage of the psychoanalysand to the psychoanalyst.

Evoked by the above developments, here is the ultimate question. How can one acknowledge that Althusser was not present in his passage to the act and affirm at the same time that, in contrast to the epic leap, the passage to the act is characterised by an "I am": an "I am" without any thought? The hypothesis of the unconscious could mistakenly offer the possibility of discarding this objection. Certainly, one could say, no conscious thought is active here. Nonetheless, it remains that unconscious thoughts were at work – all the more so, as Althusser provides information that, once studied and taken as a whole, could allow us to determine *the meaning* of his passage to the act: in other words, to inscribe it in a history, a history that would make it an epic leap. However, as intelligent and precise as they may be, we leave the reading of these "constructions" (Freud), sensing that they do not *grasp* the passage to the act but rather float above it like a cloud above a mountain peak, soon to be carried elsewhere by the wind. The very diversity of these constructions attests to the fact that none of them is final. The acknowledgement of the act refutes the imperialism of the unconscious no less than the imperialism of thought.

No thought motivated Althusser to commit the act of murder, there was no pre-meditation, admitted by both psychiatrists and judges. We now see the justness of the non-place [case dismissal], whereas a condemnation – no doubt contrary to what Althusser wished for at the time – would not have suppressed this absence from himself. *The same necessity is manifested in the truth of the non-place and in the disappearance during the murder.*

We already know the answer to this apparent aporia: it consists of one word – "disappeared". "Disappeared" implies both the absence in the act and the "I am" (the one who has disappeared) that is characteristic of the passage to the act.

The murder of the hallucinated Hélène or of the hallucination of Hélène could be seen as an epic leap. Possessed as Althusser was by the intention of making her alive,[42] it has a meaning – it is inscribed in a history. However, in this act there is another and a different act "Come!", for which Hélène is only a support: the "Come!" that would made exist the sexual relation. This affirmation is confirmed, if not established, by a statement made by Jacques Lacan:

> Things are such that, that given that this year I am aiming to speak to you of *the One*, I shall begin today by articulating the relevance of this to the Other [*l'Autre*] ... the Other, with a capital O, with regard to which I gathered – some time ago – the concern marked by a Marxist to whom I owed the place from which I was able to take up my work once again: his concern was that the Other was a third which, in putting it forward in relation to the couple, he (the Marxist) could identify it only as God.[43]

Claude Lévi-Strauss had already made the observation to Lacan that God could well be found there, under the cover of the Other. However, there is more here, according to Lacan's statement: the positioning of the Other could have been linked to the couple as far as Althusser was concerned. "Couple": the term crystallises the tyranny of "being two", as was so clearly established by Guy Hocquenghem.[44] Today, we do not think so much of the union, of making *One* from *Two,* as of making a couple, of being a couple, of coupling. In both cases, what is at work is the thought, the belief or the illusion of the existence of the sexual relation. Reconnecting with his former Catholicism, Althusser could only make this couple exist through a divine third. That is, I would say, his seriousness, one that was recently confirmed by the publication of *Aveux de la chair* by Michel Foucault.[45] There is no more tangible proof that this famous couple does not exist – any more than the sexual relation that Althusser's passage to the act tries to make exist, like a mirage in the desert.

Let us now return to the theatre, with yet another question. This auditorium, experienced as empty, the place of an allocution that is lacking: was not the same place where God is expected and questioned? The day after Althusser and Lacan had dinner together for the first time, on 4 December 1963, Althusser wrote Lacan a rather long letter – which, no doubt, remained without any response, as if that silence were already announcing the empty auditorium that was, for me, so engaging and important. From it, I extract two statements – "Yes, there is Outside. Thank God."[46] One may read, "Yes, there is, outside, a God. Thanks." (*"Oui, il y a un Dehors. Dieu merci."* ... *"Oui, il y a, dehors, un Dieu. Merci."*)

Three years later, dedicating his *Écrits* to Louis Althusser, Lacan wrote: "Here we are, in the same boat".[47] This is doubtful.

Notes

1. In the same way as Marguerite Duras speaking with Manon (see p. 000 below), Carlos Busqued extensively interviewed Ricardo Melogno, who was confined in a psychiatric hospital after having committed four remarkably similar murders. A book resulted from this: *Magnetizado. Una conversación con Ricardo Melogno*, published in Barcelona (Editorial Anagrama, 2018, not yet translated into French). These kinds of books offer an invaluable perspective on madness, particularly of cases involving murder, when the writer's relationship with the person being interviewed is free of any therapeutic purpose. What happens is that the writers (Duras, Busqued) gather words other than those spoken to medical staff.
2. *L'Avenir dure longtemps. Le testament d'Althusser* (Paris, Maison des Métallos, 20–25 March 2018). Louis Althusser, *L'Avenir dure longtemps* (1992), edition presented by Olivier Corpet and Yann Moulier-Boutang (Paris, Flammarion, 2013).
3. This could constitute a proposal for a recurrence.
4. This [audience] could have *once* [*un temps*] taken the form of Jacques Lacan, if Louis Althusser had chosen him as his psychoanalyst. As we know, this did not happen even though there is hardly any doubt that, if anyone incarnated the analyst for Althusser, it was none other than Jacques Lacan, his "*analyste d'élection*" ("analyst of choice", according to a very astute designation by Conrad Stein, who observed that some demands for analysis avoid addressing the one who, nonetheless, is recognised as analyst, indeed as the analyst par excellence, by the one making the demand). I presented and discussed this trait in *Louis Althusser récit divan* (Paris, Epel, 1992).
5. Book of Apocalypse, xx, 14.
6. This was well known to the families of the "disappeared" who were thrown into the sea by the French army during the Algerian war. This new method of disappearance was then taught to the Argentine army when Argentina's political regime was a dictatorship.
7. "*Au centre du texte, un voyage*", text published on the IMEC website on the occasion of Louis Althusser's centenary (he was born in 1918): www.imec.archives. com.fr.
8. This disparate list brings together places, a state (tactfully called "illness") and an action, whereas the psychiatric hospital is absent from it.
9. Notably, Alain de Libera, *L'Invention du sujet modern* (Paris, Vrin, 2015).
10. The third edition consists of 543 *bons mots* [quips, witty remarks]: *Les impromptus de Lacan* (Paris, Fayard, 2009).
11. Lacan hardly felt obliged to declare the reasons for his short sessions. He did so, at least once, in mentioning an analysand who occupied his sessions by talking about the news, films and literature.
12. "I always had an extreme desire to learn to distinguish the true from the false, to see clearly in my actions and to walk confidently through this life" (*Discourse on the Method, Part 1*).
13. For a more detailed discussion of this *vel*, please refer to Chapter III of this work.
14. Jacques Lacan, "*L'instance de la lettre dans l'inconscient*", Sorbonne, Paris, 9 May 1957.
15. In Jacques Lacan, *Écrits* (Paris, Éditions du Seuil, 1966, p. 517). An attentive reader could quite rightly note, as did Inès Crespo, that I am taking all of – as if they were the same, the logical operator "*ou, ou*" ["or, or"] and the locative/temporal adverb, "*où, où*" ["where, where", the only difference in French being a grave accent on *u* of the latter], to the point where one may imagine that a single statement of two different sentences were successively quoted above. Homophones invite this, but so does the configuration of numerous schemas that Lacan invented and used in two successive seminars: *La Logique du fantasme*, 1996–1997 and *L'Acte*

psychanalytique, 1967–1968). Place (topological) and choice (logical) cannot be conceived independently from each other when the place inserts a choice in a net (the whole of a schema), which specifies and orders the value and meaning of each choice. Two different places demand that the "*ou bien, ou bien*" ["either or"] "can only be mutually exclusive.

16 Jacques Lacan, *La Logique du fantasme*, seminar, 11 January, 1967.
17 The session of 27 May 1964 (*Les Quatre Concepts fondamenteaux de la psychanalyse*) presented in detail the configuration named "*vel* of alienation". The alternative thus concerned being and meaning.
18 Published by Juan Pablo Luccheli in his work *Lacan, De Wallon à Kojève* (Paris, Éditions Michele, 2017).
19 Jacques Lacan, *L'Identification*, Roussan's version (by far the most trustworthy). [*Translator's note*: Some of Lacan's seminars were recorded, creating different recordings with different recording points, and with a change of tapes at different points. Hence there can be different sources for the same seminar.]
20 Maurice Blanchot, *Thomas l'Obscur*, (new version, Paris, Gallimard, 1950, pp. 109–116). I owe to Alfrédo López the reminder of this reference, and I thank him for it here.
21 Among Descartes scholars, there is agreement on the eminently punctual character of the *cogito*. It is only true in the moment that someone somehow repeats it on his own behalf. In other words: one cannot deduce from "I think, therefore I am" that "I am a thinking being". Thus, Lacan was able to see a passage to the act in the *punctual* moment when a subject, because he observes himself thinking, recognises that he is.
22 Marguerite Duras, *L'Amante anglaise* (Paris, Gallimard, 1967, p. 115).
23 In this context, the image of the capital letter V serves as a medium for the actions. Cf. Guy Casadamont, "*Althusser derrière là le V en masse*", *Quid pro quo*, no. 4 (Paris, Epel, 2009).
24 Francis Dupré, *La "Solution" du passage à l'acte. Le double crime des sœurs Papin* (Toulouse, Érès, 1984). Quite recently, there has been renewed interest in the Papin sisters. Two programmes on France Culture were devoted to them on 15 and 16 December 2018, a sign that the issue is not over.
25 Arthur Rimbaud, *Le Bateau Ivre* [written in 1871; for translation, see University of Chicago Press, 2005, p. 129).
26 Jacques Lacan, *Le Désir et son interpretation*, 22 April 1959. (See *Pas-tout Lacan*, https://ecole-lacanienne.net/bibliolacan/pas-tout-lacan/.)
27 Louis Althusser, *L'Avenir dure longtemps* (1992) (Paris, Flammarion, 2013, p. 242).
28 Louis Althusser, *L'Avenir dure longtemps* (1992) (Paris, Flammarion, 2013, emphasis by Althusser).
29 Imagine Marina's joy (see p. 42) if she had received a word from her missing fiancé ... Marina, with whom I must have been infatuated at just five years old in order to have observed her so carefully (a remark graciously offered to the psychoanalyst who is a firm believer in the nuclear character of the Oedipus complex).
30 Emphasis by Althusser.
31 Roland Barthes, *Le Neutre. Cours au Collège de France (1977–1978)* (Paris, Éditions du Seuil/Imec, 2002).
32 Paul Valéry, "La pythie", in *Charmes* [1922] (Paris, Gallimard, 1953). I quoted this poem for the first time while studying Lacan's view of Irma's injection (*Érotique du deuil au temps de la mort sèche* [1995] (second edition, Paris, Epel, 1997, pp. 102–107).
33 Louis Althusser, *L'Avenir dure longtemps* (1992) (Paris, Flammarion, 2013, p. 34).

34 See Anne-Marie Vindras, *Robert Gaupp, un monster et son psychiatre* (Paris, Epel, 1996). Also, *Louis II de Bavière selon Ernst Wagner paranoïque dramturge* (Paris, Epel, 1993). *Délire*, the play written by Ernst Wagner remains, as far as I k now, the only case in which a paranoic created a theatrical work about another paranoic.
35 See Raquel Capurro, Diego Nin, *Je l'ai tué, dit-elle, c'est mon père* (translated for Spanish, Uruguay, by Françoise Ben Kemoun, Paris, Epel, 2005).
36 Passage cited by I. Fenoglio, *Une auto-graphie du tragique, Les manuscrits de Les Faits et de L'Avenir dure longtemps de Louis Althusser*, Preface by Yann Moulier-Boutang (Louvain-la-Neuve, Academia Bruyland, 2007). I found this thanks to an article by G. Casadamont, "*Althusser derrière là le V en masse*", *Quid pro quo*, no. 4 (Paris, Epel, 2009).
37 Word scribbled out to the point of being almost illegible.
38 The forward slash was drawn by hand on the typescript.
39 Louis Althusser, *Écrits philosophiques et politiques*, t.I, texts gathered and presented by François Matheron, Paris, Stock/Imec, 1994, republished, 1999, p. 550-551. I found this thanks to G. Casadamont, "Althusser derrière là le V en masse", article cited.
40 This is not at all a case of a face-to-face, of a link that some would qualify as "narcissistic". Hélène both *occupies* the place of the Other and *incarnates* the Other, which was qualified above as "double presence". I believed it necessary to propose a term so that the very banal situation in which a subject chooses a partner should no longer be neglected: "incarpation", a condensation of "incarnation" and "occupation" (*L'Autresexe*, Paris, Epel, 2015, p. 183). Incarnation: doomed to cease, something remains contingent. Occupation: a foreign army occupies a country, takes it over, appropriates the decisions that its inhabitants would usually make. Incarpation is not to be seen as being close to repression, denial, reactional formation, foreclosure, or sublimation: operations that the subject somehow realises upon himself (at least, in the ways that these are thought of). Incarpation is the name of what occurs erotically when someone is vested in his/her partner.
41 Please see note 40 above, as here we have the interplay of incarnation and occupation.
42 We noted the presence of this trait in the jihadist act (see above, p. 000). It is only accessible if one is told that physical death is not the last word in one's destiny, and that physical death opens a space: the space between-two-deaths (Jacques Lacan, *L'Éthique de la psychanalyse*, session of 6 July 1960). For a more detailed account of this space, please refer to Chapter II in Jean Allouch, *La Scène lacanienne et son cercle magique* (Paris, Epel, 2017).
43 Jacques Lacan, ... *ou pire*, session of 8 March 1972.
44 Guy Hocquenghem, "*L'Avenir du couple*", *Libération*, 22 August 1980, republished in *Chimères*, no. 69. For a more extensive development of this point, please see Jean Allouch, *L'Autresexe* (Paris, Epel, 2015, p. 105, n. 63).
45 Michel Foucault, *Histoire de la sexualité*, IV, Foreword by Frédéric Gros (Paris, Gallimard 2018).
46 Louis Althusser, *Écrits sur la psychanalyse. Freud et Lacan* (Paris, Stock/Imec, 1993, p. 285).
47 Louis Althusser, *Écrits sur la psychanalyse. Freud et Lacan* (Paris, Stock/Imec, 1993, p. 270, copy of the dedication).

Chapter III

Passage to the act and the epic leap: Marguerite Duras

In 1968, Marguerite Duras wrote a play of her novel *L'Amante anglaise* (1967): *Le Théâtre de l'Amante anglaise*.[1] At the same time, numerous elements of *Les Viaducs de la Seine-et-Oise*, a play written in 1959 and first performed in 1963, were taken up and reconfigured. Here is the last statement of a brief passage from *Les Viaducs ...*, read just before the curtain is raised: "The combined efforts of the law and the perpetrators fail to come up with any reasons for this crime. The crime thus remains unexplained."[2] The audience is immediately alerted that this is about something other than providing an explanation. What, then? It is about offering the possibility of joining the magic circle of those who are interested in what took place between the murderer and her victim, and between the victim and her murderer.[3] And this is your place, too, you who have this page in front of you, simply because you are reading it.

Nothing that can be said or written about this crime will ever be able to fill the hole that is so neatly indicated by the lack of an explanation. Or, more precisely still, no matter what statement is made, it will only have meaning if it is struck by – that is, if it is the carrier of – this trait: the radical absence of explanation. Any statement about the murder will be *tenuous*, not *tendered* [*ténu*, not *tenu*]: it will leave its place to the act, as act. This mark is permanently present in Duras' literary work, at least since *Le Ravissement de Lol V. Stein*, published in 1964, one year after *Les Viaducs ...*, and three years before *L'Amante anglaise*. In 1962, Doctor Le Guillan invited Marguerite Duras to spend a whole day with a woman called Manon, outside the walls of the psychiatric hospital where she was confined – a woman whom, for years, Duras could not get out of her mind. What followed this meeting was the writing of *Le Ravissement ...* We do not know why Doctor Le Guillan gave Duras such an unusual invitation. During the post-war years, Duras welcomed to her Parisian home in Rue Saint-Benoît many of the "beau monde" – including Jacques Lacan. Whether she entertained them well or promised them fame, Claude Roy had no hesitation in calling her the queen of "the Saint-Benoît group". Lacan said something different, acknowledging her as delightful (*ravisseuse*) and himself as delighted (*ravi*) by her; not, however, in the sense in which Lol was delighted [*ravie*]. Lacan's *"Hommage fait à Marguerite Duras du Ravissement de Lol*

V. Stein", published in 1965, took the work out of the "coffin" where it was buried as soon as it had appeared (as Duras said). For her part, Duras was not at all delighted (*ravie*) by Lacan. Nonetheless, they had a shared trait: that is, the fundamental absence of explanation which, without impairing in any way their (literary, clinical, theoretical) writing, is in keeping with its object.[4] [*Translator's note*: The "shared trait": no explanation is essential in psychoanalysis.] What object? Madness. About which, any explanation that is not struck by its own suspension of judgement (*épokhē*) is inappropriate.

Reminder

Almost all the pieces of the deaf-mute Marie-Thérèse Bousquet's corpse were thrown by her murderer onto several freight trains passing beneath the Viorne viaduct and were thus dispersed. The task was difficult and burdensome: it took three nights and nine trips back and forth.

Just as we noted previously with regard to the jihadists of 9/11, this act, too, was signed[5] – by two words written on different surfaces: one was "Alfonso", on the wall of the cellar where the dismemberment took place, and the other was "Cahors" (joined to "Alfonso", a man with whom the murderer was in love) on the pieces of the corpse (p. 47). The novel provides a key to understanding each of these two inscriptions. We will later discuss the meaning of the inscription on the pieces of the body. The inscription "Alfonso" in the cellar comes in the place of a cry, an inexpressible cry for help addressed to Alfonso.

> Because I could not cry out, as this would have awoken my husband, I therefore wrote? Perhaps. I do not remember. It came to me to write in order to call out, even though I knew that it was futile.
>
> (p. 178)

All the pieces of the corpse were found, except for the head. Claire Lannes never says precisely where it is. Moreover, she does not respond when she is questioned (p. 45), a position that is no longer partly hers once her murderous act is acknowledged, almost in a lapsus, and in order to prevent anyone from following the wrong track (pp. 43–127).

We know, therefore, quite early on that Claire Lannes committed the murder and who the victim was: so, the question that arises, as we continue to read the novel, is the banal and common one that almost goes without saying: what are the motives for this crime? We also wonder: who is this woman, who committed the murder, and the dismemberment and dispersal of her victim's corpse?

Gradually, however, the questions come down to just one: "Why was the head treated so differently?"

Marguerite Duras did not invent *ex nihilo* the absence of the head for the recomposition of the body. She had read the account of the trial of Amélie

Rabilloux, published in *Le Monde*, 1 March 1952, and then investigated further (the Rabilloux case initiated and inspired Duras' three connected works: *Les Viaducs de Seine-et-Oise*, *L'Amante anglaise* and *Le Théâtre de l'Amante anglaise*):

> What we blame Amélie Rabilloux for, what we want to understand in her crime, is not so much the killing of her husband, but the fact that she then dismembered his corpse and went and spread its pieces in the drains and empty fields of Savigny-sur-Orge. But she was incapable of clearly [*clairement*] explaining this.[6]

Could it be that the metamorphosis of "Amélie" to "Claire" is due to the word "clearly" [*clairement*]? Claire's words are clear, to the point of bringing clarity to the extreme limits against which explanation crashes and fails. This passage of the article in *Le Monde*, by Jean-Marc Théolleyre, does not mention that some pieces of the dismembered husband's corpse were thrown from the top of the so-called "Montagne Pavée" viaduct.

Figure 3.1 The viaduct of the Montagne Pavée from which Amélie threw the pieces of her husband's body onto freight trains (p. 75).

Nor does it mention that the murdered husband's ears were never found.[7] Nonetheless, the article hints at the enigmatic absence of these ears. During the trial of the accused, writes Théolleyre, "beneath the featureless cheek, under the yellowish skin and just against the ear, the muscle periodically contracted, like a tic". In *L'Amante anglaise*, it is the whole head that fails to appear in the recomposition of the victim's body.

The discussion of this astonishing absence takes place, and yet the problem is never resolved. Duras wished this to be so, hoping to reserve "part of the book for the reader to do" (p. 10). We play this Durasian game that, according to her, "always exists", no matter what book is involved (and here we think of Lacan, as he also knew how to reserve "part for the reader"), by soon proposing a solution to the mystery: a solution that will not dispel the mystery but will approach it a little more closely.

The epic leap in *L'Amante anglaise*

As we will later confirm, the first part of the novel presents itself like the account of an epic leap. We can see that it is similar to those already evoked: the jihadist act (Chapter I), the acts of Iris Cabeduzo, Ernst Wagner and others of the same kind (Chapter II). At the beginning of the novel, it is Pierre Lannes, Claire's husband, who speaks – or, more precisely, it is his voice recorded on a tape recorder during a meeting at the *Le Balto* café. Present at the meeting are Robert Lamy (the owner of the café), Alfonso Rignieri, Pierre Lannes, a man who is attempting (poorly) to hide his status as a police officer, barely concealing his own tape recorder, a young woman who is new in the company of these regulars,[8] and Claire Lannes – who is initially absent (this is astonishing) and who, we soon learn, is someone who is fierce and hard.[9] A second tape recorder, the police officer's, records what can be heard on the tape recording being played and the remarks that accompany this group listening *in vivo*. Seen as a whole, this arrangement (graphically conveyed in the novel) is a *mise en abime*. The voice of Pierre Lannes:

"Basically, the cause of most crimes is, perhaps, merely finding oneself faced with the possibility of committing them. Suppose that you live day and night, for example, next to an explosive device ... and that all you have to do to set it off, is to press a button. So, one day, you do it. Suppose you live with someone for years and years and then, one evening, the idea comes to you. You tell yourself at first that if the idea came to you, you could do it – without having any intention of doing it, of course. Then you tell yourself that someone else in your place could do it, someone else who has reasons to do it. And later still, you tell yourself that you always have reasons to do it and that in your place, someone else less ..."
"Weak?"
(We do not know who interrupts Pierre Lannes: it's an "it-is-said", an "it doesn't matter who speaks".)

"Weak is certainly the word: someone else less weak than you would do it. That's how it begins. And the idea keeps coming back to you more and more often and, then, it is there, and there is remains. It grows and grows, it fills the house, you keep bumping into it. So, that's it."
"What's he saying?" (Claire, addressing Alfonso.)
"A load of rubbish."
"And then, one day, you do it. Afterwards – that's another story."

An epic leap, therefore: considered in advance, somehow foreseen, and not in any way a disruption. The episodes in an epic make sense. We see this in Homer, the founder of epic literature in the West.[10] The name Homer has been made into an adjective. "Homeric anger" is an anger that is famous, intense and acknowledged as being worthy of Homer: it is inscribed in a story, the mode of expression of which is the epic (the *Robert* dictionary proposes "epic" as equivalent to "Homeric"). The epic leap does not present the unpredictability, absurdity, non-sense and surprise that the passage to the act constitutes for everyone, beginning with whoever has committed it. Paradigmatic of the passage to the act and in contrast to the epic leap, are the crimes of the Papin sisters and Althusser – at least according to the trait we have just recalled, as Althusser's action also comes within the realm of the epic leap. As for Claire Lannes – to see in her case, as has been said, an epic leap, would be to ignore a remark of Pierre Lannes, her husband "Perhaps a minute before killing her, she did not think that she was going to kill her" (p. 115). Except for the word "perhaps", this sentence appears to contradict what Pierre Lannes says in the above quotation. We shall come back later to the difficulty that was already raised with regard to Althusser's act (Chapter II, pp. 54–58).

As a consequence of the incomprehensible and inexplicable nature of the passage to the act, something that I have named *effet-d'entre*[11] (between-effect) comes into play, no doubt more intensely than anywhere else. We wonder: what happened *between* the Papin sisters and their landladies? And *between* Louis Althusser and Hélène Rytmann? And we can also refer to Lacan, interrogating the cascade of between (*entre*) in a poem by Antoine Tudal,[12] which interested him so much as he endeavoured to better understand love, and the gap between man and woman that is so effectively conveyed by the reboundings of *entre* (*between*) in the poem.[13] All around a passage to the act, is the "magic circle" of those who, as if magnetised by the *effet-d'entre*, can do nothing other than get closer to it, as it is also a matter of their own questioning. Lacanians also form a magic circle that gathers those who wonder what happened *between* Jacques Lacan and his *thing* – which is not Freudian in all its aspects.

Further: what is happening *between* the parents of a child who surprises them in bed while they are …? The said "primitive scene" is, no doubt, most especially the carrier of the *effet-d'entre*. Lacan could have had this in mind when, on 8 March 1972 (… *ou pire*), he was preparing to "unveil" (!) "what's happening with regard to this Other," his own then. He began by stating that "the Other is the Other of the sexual couple" even if it is that Other with whom one does not *jouir* sexually. How can these two statements be reconciled? I see no other way of doing so but by distinguishing two different analytics of sex: the Other is sexualised, but without enjoying sexually. This tension calls for a response and even an invention – nothing less than a new definition of the Other. Lacan: "*The Other, understand this well (!), is therefore an Entre: the Entre that the sexual relation is about, but displaced to precisely s'Autreposer*"[14] (from the verb *entreposer*: to deposit, to keep, to stock, to the neologism composed of *autre* and *poser* in the form of a reflexive verb). This Other comes between, intervenes, interposes – which produces an effect: the *effet-d'entre*.[15] Lacan came back to this "entre" several times.[16] On 9 October 1974,[17] he stated that he could never reach "the resolution of the relation between the *parlêtres* (speaking-beings) that we sex as male and the *parlêtres* that we sex as woman.[18] One year later, on 14 October 1975, he added this "entre" to the account of his own "*tentrisme*" (his *entre*, his erotic) to the extent of mistreating and deforming French with the phrase "*je t'entre*" ["I between/enter you"]. It was at this time that the *entre* became crucial – not only because the absence of something (notably the phallus) that would make a link between man and woman permits the affirmation of the non-existence of the sexual relation, but also because the *entre* is at the heart of the Borromean knot: "The three that are there function as pure consistency: that is, it is only in holding together that they consist" (17 December 1974).

For all those who turned towards the murder of Marie-Thérèse Bousquet, it was not just a matter of explaining the murder, but also a matter of the shock evoked by its extreme violence, which was immediately perceived to have occurred – a violence that was somehow supplementary. Durassian before the term existed, Jean-Marc Théolleyre wrote (we read) that the issue for everyone was not so much the murder of Rabilloux, the husband, but the dismemberment and dispersal of his corpse. Similarly, in *L'Amante anglaise*, the question that arises is not merely the act of murder but the cutting up (the "butchery") of the victim's corpse and, then, the disappearance of the head and, finally, the place where the head is. Echoing the statement of Christine Papin, "My crime is too big for me to say what it is",[19] we have the statement of Claire Lannes: "It was so hard for me to do that I cannot think of it" (p. 165). *A doing without thinking, without thoughts.*

These words distinguish the *passage to the act* from the *epic leap*. The jihadist thinks of his action, as we have seen, in several terms: the thought of his action is part of its execution and is necessary to it. In contrast, the passage to the act dispenses with all thought, *a fortiori* of all thought that can be thought.

"Either I do not think, or I am not": Lacan

The passage to the act/epic leap distinction cross-references an alternative in which the barred subject S(barred from the outset by this very choice, which constrains him) finds himself stuck – according to Lacan – without any effective possibility of escape. This alternative is the aforementioned "alienating *vel*" that Lacan qualifies as "necessary", "forced" and "inevitable": "Either I do not think, or I am not." We proposed earlier (Chapter II, pp. 46–47) an initial approach to the *vel* of alienation as Lacan presented it, and then explored and exploited it. He represented his dismembering of the negativised *cogito* by using a schema in the style of Augustus de Morgan (18 January 1967).

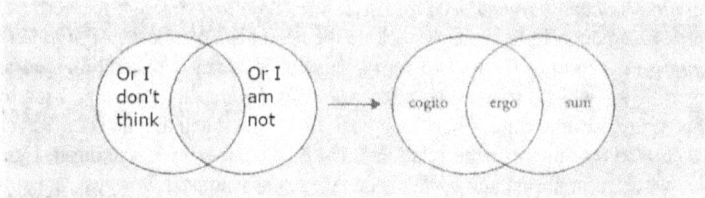

Figure 3.2 Schéma 1.

Schéma 1 is intended to represent one of Morgan's laws, according to which the union of two negated ensembles (negation of "I think" and negation of "I am") is equal to the negation of their intersection: ㄱ A v ㄱ B ~ ㄱ (A & B). As a matter of equivalence, the arrow in the centre is supposed to indicate the double meaning.

Several other schemas were produced by Lacan – richer and perhaps too full of data – that specified, with some irregularities (*work in progress?*), how the constraint of the alienating *vel* presents itself for the subject. He indicated this on 14 December 1966. The inspiration came to him from his reading of an article published in November 1966 in no. 246 of *Les Temps modernes*: "The meaning of the word structure in Mathematics."[20] Lacan said that the article, while neglecting any mention of its author Marc Barbut, "could be extended but, in the short form chosen, chews through things with extreme care: twenty-four pages through which we proceed, step by step. This is nonetheless a useful exercise for those who like length, and an exercise that could soften you towards this Klein group." Among several writings of the Klein group in this article, we take up this one: it presents an object, a white circle, from which three other objects are produced through the modification of its two characteristics (round or square) and its colour (black or white). The Klein group establishes certain (three, to be exact) connections between them:

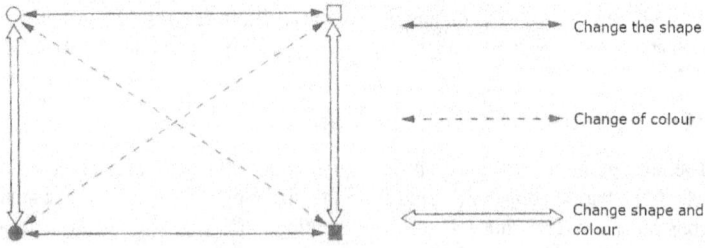

Figure 3.3 Schéma 2.

Now Lacan, no matter what has been suggested, never used the mathematical properties of the Klein group[21] as a mathematician would. François Balmès made note of this in the pages of his work[22] that he devoted to the *vel* of alienation. He observed the following. (1) While each of the Klein group's operations is involutive (repeated, each annuls itself), things are different with Lacan, where the arrows have only one direction. (2) While each apex of the Klein group can be a point of departure and a point of arrival, only one of the apices in Lacan can be a point of origin. (3) While another of the Klein group's laws means that the result of an operation must be identical to the product of two others (for example, from the white square, you can get the black circle, either directly by the transversal line or in two operations, by passing through the black square or through the white circle), we will verify below that Lacan's schemas do not permit the application of this law (for example, neither the vertical line on the left, nor the bottom horizontal, is two-directional). (4) Most of Lacan's schemas only include one diagonal or else distinguish two diagonals, one in a full line and the other in dotted line. From all of these observations, Balmès concludes: "The diagram veers towards the schematic, and considerations of direction and content are based on the logical model."[23] Note also that the names vary: sometimes we read "schematic", sometimes "quadrangle" or "tetrahedron" and, more rarely, "device", even though none of these appears to be favoured or ends up as superior. Balmès chose "quadrangle"; I will stick to "schematic", the most neutral of the three.[24] And so it seems that in extending Lacan's barely orthodox way of "dealing with" the Klein group we don't want to be more royalist than the king or, moreover, more inventive than him. Let us begin with the partly arbitrary selection of the schematic below (*L'acte psychanalytique*, session of 17 January 1968):

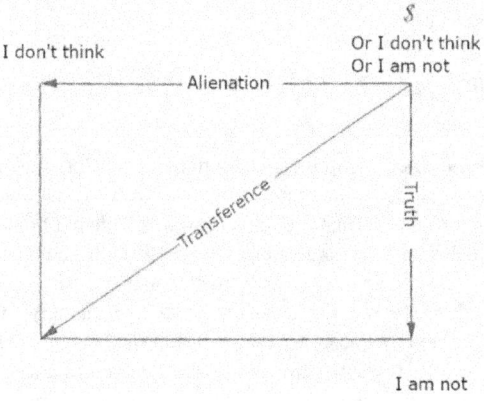

Figure 3.4 Schéma 3.

I selected this schema for its relative simplicity.[25] However, my choice could be criticised in that I decided not to study all the schemas included in this series – a choice that is all the more regrettable in that, from one schema to the other, the indications made by Lacan vary. Thus, the *"petit a"* is inscribed at the bottom left or at the top right (in one session of 17 January 1968, transcription by AFI (Association freudienne internationale) or at the bottom right (20 March, same transcription). Or the oblique line that links "I do not think" to "I am not" is acknowledged as being the line of "the task that is qualified as that of the analysand", or of castration (21 February 1968), or that of the psychoanalytic act (20 March 1968), – in which case it no longer refers to the analysand but to the analyst. These irregularities by Lacan are, moreover, accentuated by the recourse to transcribers of listeners' notes, which are sometimes incomplete or incorrect. I therefore made my choice *with hardly any other guarantee of the heuristic nature of this choice*. One would search in vain for a schema constructed on the same model that Lacan himself used and varied.

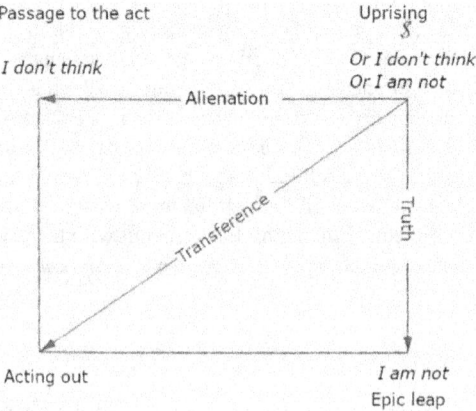

Figure 3.5 Schéma 4.

I proceeded to three "irruptive interventions". (1) "Uprising" is at the outset, above right, where Lacan placed it. The subject is constrained to choose one or the other of the alternatives: either towards "I do not think" or towards "I am not". Such a choice is *saying no* to the link established by the *cogito* between "I think" and "I am". It cannot be that of an unconscious desire or, even less so, of the desire seen as the desire of the Other. It can only be the result of an intention. Alerted by Lacan, we may be astonished here by the appearance of these two terms: "uprising" and "will". They were introduced in *La Scène lacanienne et son cercle magique*, a work to which you can refer.[26]

(2) "Acting out" has been put where Lacan had inscribed it (instead of "I do not think") because it remains defined as "transference without analysis" (Freud's *agieren*). (3) The displacement of "acting-out" leaves one place unoccupied, the place where I was thus able to put the epic leap.

The subject, barred at the outset, is not offered the choice of not choosing.[27] The subject is bound to take up his uprising, to put it into play and, as we could say with Freud, invest it: either in the place of "I do not think" which, Lacan dixit, characterises the passage to the act,[28] or in the place of the epic leap, which – because he thinks – proves *ipso facto* that he is choosing "I am not" (hence its place in Schéma 4).[29] The transference appears here as a sort of between-the-two, a kind of middle way, which offers the possibility of imagining being exempt from dealing with the alienating *vel* – to which it returns when, at the end of an analysis, the figure of a subject-supposed-to-know (not necessarily the analyst) that had offered support to the transference, is destitute.

If, in contrast to the epic leap that is thus a thinking leap, the passage to the act presents itself as an immense and mesmerising question mark, the procedure set in motion to settle this question is almost obvious: all of the case's data will be closely studied in order to produce an interpretation or, better still, a construction (Freud), which will make the passage to the act meaningful and even understandable. A notable way of avoiding the effect of the alienating *vel*, in everyone by unfailingly finding an answer that will always be ready to use. Yet this availability should in itself alone elicit some reservation with regard to its value. Or, more precisely, several answers will come to light but not one of them will prevail to the extent of eliminating the other constructions (this is also exemplified here by the case of the Papin sisters).

This final and shaky situation is one of the elements that leads to attempting something other than the path of interpretation, which is supposed to be capable (but not always] of bringing the passage to the act into the fold of the epic leap. Not neglecting this path, but by taking it to the point where it is revealed to fail, we will keep in mind – with regard to *L'Amante anglaise* – the epic leap/passage to the act distinction in order to assert the irreducibility of both the passage to the act and the epic leap. Moreover, distinguishing them from each other is what allows us to interrogate their interplay, one compared to the other: the interplay that we have barely glimpsed so far.

A mourning

So: the disappearance of Marie-Thérèse's head. Mentioned very early on, this disappearance is all the more notable in that the story keeps it away from all verbal exchanges – and thus it is silently very present. When pressed to explain herself about it, Claire Lannes ends up by dropping a few bits of information: "I made her disappear (she says about her crime) like a person who should have had her whole head" (p. 165). An equivocation resonates, reasons [*résonne, raisonne*]: who, then, should have had her whole head? Claire (of whom one wonders if she is mad)? Or Marie-Thérèse (who did, well and truly, lose her head)? Impossible to decide. However, no one could state that Claire had lost her head when she consents to say:

> As for the head, I did what was necessary. I had a hard time. Even more than the rest. I don't know if I will say where the head is ... I took care of the head last, one night. When everything was finished. I did what one usually does. I searched for a long time what to do with the head. I didn't come up with anything. So I went to Paris. I went down to the Porte d'Orléans station and I kept walking until I could find what to do. I found what to do.
> (pp. 138–139)

Later (p. 184), she gives details about what she has done with the head, but she does not ever say where the head was put:

> I made a burial for it/her [in French, "head" takes the feminine gender so that the pronoun here, *elle*, could refer to either the head or the victim]. [Another equivocation? *Elle*, the head? Yes, no doubt. But also *elle*, Marie-Thérèse.] And I said my prayer for the dead. I couldn't find anything else even though the agent of Cahors separated me from God and I never found him again [found whom again? the agent of Cahors? God?].

A mourning ritual then, but without *publikum*, without a "magic circle"[30] – at the moment at least, because having described this ritual Duras has her readers beside her and, together, they form a magic circle. The religious hue does not allow any doubt to remain, even though we initially could not see, right at the beginning of the novel (p. 26), that it had already been clearly announced.

Claire Lannes' reconnecting with God at this moment takes her back to the agent of Cahors.[31] She has spent her life loving this "superb man", by whom she was loved for two years ("we were madly in love with each other"). He left his wife for her, and she renounced God for him, to the point that he took the place of God for her (p. 152). We think of Marguerite Anzieu, Lacan's Aimée, who wrote this poem in her novel, *Le Détracteur*:

> Prenez ma main je vous la donne
> Car depuis que je vous ai vu
> Je n'aime plus Dieu de même
> Je l'aime mieux, je l'aime moins
> Est-ce vous ou bien lui que j'aime

Sans doute vous êtes le même

Take my hand I give it to you
For ever since I saw you
I don't love God the same
I love him more, I love him less
Is it you or him I love
No doubt you are the same[32].

While for Marguerite Anzieu, God and her *poétereau* (unremarkable poet) were "the same", even though a doubt remains in this identification, Claire Lannes substituted the second for the first.

> It was he who separated me from God. I saw only him after God. I listened only to him; he was everything to me and one day I no longer had God, but him alone.
> (p. 153)

This goes on until the moment when, as she realises that the agent of Cahors has just lied to her, the substitution collapses. However, this collapse does not result in a return to God. Devastated, she attempts to end her life (p. 95).

Similarly to God, the agent of Cahors does not have a name that is his own; he is designated only by *his function* as agent of Cahors. This lets us understand that, right to the end, the wish that he could be a substitute for God, a substitute that leaves her without God, persists in Claire Lannes.

While the agent of Cahors and God – from whom the former inherited certain traits – are present in Claire Lannes' mind at the moment of the mourning ritual when she explicitly reconnects with God, he was not absent during the murder and the dispersal of the pieces of body. As this last trait has nothing evident, it is appropriate to substantiate it.

Of what institution or business is the so-called "agent of Cahors" an agent? Is he an agent of the police, as affirmed by the police investigator questioning Robert Lamy (p. 63)? The qualification "of the police" would then be repeated forever in the novel, which does not cease to call him "the agent of Cahors", a qualification that was not taken up in *Le Théâtre de l'Amante anglaise*. Each time, it would suffice to add "of the police" to "agent of Cahors", to therefore write "the agent of the police of Cahors" (two genitives in a row – Flaubert gave chase to this succession) in order to strike a fatal blow to Marguerite Duras' style. Is he an agent of Post, Telegraphs and Telephones? An agent of a bank? I would propose that he is an agent of the SNCF [*Société nationale de Chemins de fer* – French National Railway Company]. Many things then fall into place. However, this does not mean that everything can be understood because, on the contrary, the specification of his professional status makes the two actions of Claire Lannes all the more strange: on the one hand, the murder and what follows and, on the other, the mourning ritual, which cannot be placed under the same insignia as the action of cutting up the body and then throwing the pieces of it off the parapet of a viaduct.

The thread is too thick to be explicit. When Emmanuel Finkiel came out of the first screening of his film, *La Douleur*, he agreed to an interview with *Le Monde* (24 January 2018). Here are his closing words:

> I detested Duras while working on my film. Then, I was reconquered. Her threads are too thick. She shows us that she is lying. She exposes her weakness to better show us the truth.

Here, we shall distinguish the thread with the help of a detour through *Les Viaducs de Seine-et-Oise*, in which Claire and Marcel Ragond, murderers of Thérèse, who was deaf-mute, retirees of the SNCF. Of course, this initial clue in itself would not prove much ... if it were not for the previously mentioned news of the crime, which inspired the play and which Duras presented as follows:

> The people were called the Rabilloux. He was a retired member of the military. She had never had any fixed employment. They had two children: two daughters. The crime was committed by the Rabilloux wife on the person of her husband. One evening, while he was reading the newspaper, she broke his skull with the mason's hammer, used to split firewood. After the crime, Amèlie Rabilloux spent several nights dismembering the corpse. Then, at night, she threw the pieces of the corpse onto freight trains that went under the Montagne Pavée viaduct, at a rate of one piece per train each night.[33]

Les Viaducs changes the military man of the news article to an agent of the SNCF. In the article that the *Pléiade* devoted to the play, it says that (as quoted by Duras) the woman "threw pieces of the body from the viaduct onto trains that were going through Savigny-sur-Orge; they were found in Lille, Bordeaux and in Cahors".[34] At the station of Cahors where, according to my conjecture, the agent of the SNCF worked. Another significant change in the play from the news: "Rabilloux" becomes "Ragond", which – among other signifiers – allows us to hear "wagon".

We shall go further with this conjecture, which could be recognised as *delirant*, (from Latin *delirare*: to go off the furrow), in the sense of *Les Folies raisonnantes* of Sérieux and Capgras. A viaduct crosses over a railway line. It is unlikely that this crossing takes place precisely above the collection of switch points, which, in sending trains in different directions, permitted – by means of railway intersections – the pinpointing of the town of Viorne in *L'Amante anglaise* as the place where the murder was committed. And so, let us turn to the more credible case in which the viaduct is above a railway track that goes in two directions, as we can observe in the photograph of the Montagne Pavée viaduct. There are only two possible directions: one in which the trains, having passed under the viaduct, are sent to different destinations by railway intersections; the other in which the trains are directed in only one direction. Which one? It is towards Cahors that the trains passing through Savigny-sur-Orge are directed.

Another detail is to be added to this Freud-Holmes investigation. There is no city or town in France that is called "Viorne". However, "Viorne" or "Viosne" is the name of a tributary of the River Oise, which flows into the Seine. Two possibilities present themselves to anyone who wishes to send pieces of a human body far away: the river or the freight train. Claire Lannes: "I didn't think of the viaduct. I went towards the river and I passed beneath it." The choice of the train was not thought of or anticipated in advance: it was while she was walking, burdened for the first time by one or more pieces of the corpse, that the idea of the train came to Claire Lannes, like an *Einfall* [as a thought].

Written in charcoal (easily accessible in the cellar), the pieces of the body carried the inscription composed of two words "Alfonso" and "Cahors" (p. 47). A name, a place: it's a postal address, which does not seem incomplete if it is true that, according to my conjecture, the agent of Cahors worked at the SNCF station at Cahors. The fact that some of the pieces of the corpse were found at other destinations does not mean that Cahors was not their intended destination. The pieces of corpse are, as it were, letters (Claire wrote many) that – following Lacan – can be recognised as destined to go somewhere to someone. Where? Cahors. Someone? The agent of Cahors whose work assigned him to the SNCF station of Cahors. He remains forever her only, persistent and unrequited great love.

The interest of this conjecture lies in the fact that it offers new information for the analysis of Claire Lannes' acts (we began by distinguishing two: epic leap and passage to the act). *Among others, they are the chosen bias for a letter to reach the agent of Cahors. Chosen ...* in vain because she does not know that the agent of Cahors, like the God of Nietzsche, is deceased.

This letter is a letter of love, of a carnal love that Claire Lannes knows is both living and foreclosed.[35] She cannot get used to it – the survival of a love that is definitely lost, even though at her own initiative she tore herself away from the arms of the agent of Cahors during a final rendezvous in Paris.[36] What was he invited to know, the agent of Cahors, as he discovered in a wagon of merchandise a piece of flesh on which were written two words, "Cahors" and Alfonso"? If he had been alive, which she believed, and somehow extra perceptive, as she thought him to be, he would have read in "Cahors" a reminder of the former love of which he was the object and, in "Alfonso", the name of someone who is revealed as incapable of replacing him. However, this letter did not reach its destination: it fell into the hands of the police. Whoever has read "The seminar on 'the purloined letter'" is no longer ignorant of the fact that the police can hardly be the ultimate destination of a letter. Is it up to the reader of *L'Amante anglaise* (and not just up to Marguerite Duras) to place him or herself where – God being absent as well – this letter would find its true destination?

What could the effect of this letter be on a love that could be qualified as "pure love" because it endures even after the lover has been rejected? The letter is a conclusive moment in a story: the story of a love for God, then for a man who is finally revealed as not being a substitute for God. Can a pure love choose a human being? We shall come to ask whether, rather than seeing the sending of this letter as part of the passage to the act, it would be better to see in it one of the characteristic traits of the epic leap. In effect, this letter takes its place in a love story, in a narrative, even though the meaning and manner of the sending of it remains partly obscure.

We are thus led to distinguish, on the one hand, the sending of this letter and the special treatment of the head as pertaining to an epic leap and, on the other hand, the murder of Marie-Thérèse and the violence done to her corpse as pertaining to the passage to the act. The sending of the letter and the burial of the head are part of one action, which is both erotic and spiritual. Ultimately, it is to God that this letter is addressed: to the God who once became man, the agent of Cahors – different, it is true, from the crucified Christ – the God to whom, after her action (both passage to the act and epic leap), Claire Lannes can pray once again, as he made a mourning ritual possible for her.

The letter comes to recall the love for God, the love that Claire Lannes renounces by engaging in the mourning ritual. The head is not only the head of Marie-Thérèse, but also Claire Lannes' head:

> In the garden, you know, I had a lead cover above my head ... Most often, ideas dropped down on me. They stayed on the lead cover, crawling all over it, and it was so painful that several times I thought of removing [my head] in order to suffer no longer.
>
> (p. 160)

In this garden, all alone, where she spent most of her time, a link had already been established between the head crawling with ideas that fell from above – thoughts that are, therefore, strictly speaking, not her own thoughts,[37] troubling, uncontrolled, unwelcome thoughts – and the death of someone: herself on this occasion. "Who were you in the garden?" – "The one who remains after my death" (p. 151). Indeed, since the agent of Cahors's lie, which divested him of his divine character, Claire Lannes is dead to love, to all life. But it will be Marie-Thérèse who dies because, if Claire really killed herself this time, all that we are dealing with, as it is all about her, could not have taken place. The mourning ritual resolves the experience of the garden. She finds herself tranquillised at last (p. 139).

Inspired and possessed by the gods, as I am surprised to be (all the responsibility for this comes back to dear Marguerite Donnadieu, her maiden name,[38] I can now specify where Claire Lannes disposed of the head, by inventing for her (*elle* the head, *elle* Marie-Thérèse Bousquet, *elle* Claire Lannes) a mourning ritual. Where? "I conducted," she says, "a whole burial for it" (p. 184). This suggests that she dug a grave for the head and covered it with earth after putting it into the hole. In Paris? Under the bitumen? "Burial" has a larger meaning: "giving a *sépulture*" or "all of the ceremonies that precede and accompany the burial" (the *Robert* dictionary). Claire Lannes went to the banks of the River Seine where they are crossed by the Saint-Michel bridge (the shortest route to the Seine from the port of Orléans). Four convergent data support this conjecture, even though they do not make it certain. (1) She arrives in Paris at the Porte d'Orléans, and then walks (as she says) to the river (as she does not say). (2) Her suicide attempt in a pond: here is water again, whereas, as we have seen, she herself is also the object of this mourning ritual. (3) She initially thought of getting rid of Marie-Thérèse's body in a river. (4) She spoke of her fear of being buried alive, hence the choice of water.

An incomplete epic leap

Claire Lannes, tranquillised, could not have been so without a certain void at the heart of her epic leap:

> What a mad woman says does not matter. So, why ask me where the head is as what I say does not matter? Perhaps I no longer know where I put it; perhaps I have forgotten the exact place? Some indication, even if it is vague, would suffice, A single word. Forest. Riverbank. – But why? – Curiosity. – So, only this word would matter among thousands of others? And do you think that I am going to let myself say this word? So that others be buried alive, and myself among them, in the asylum?
>
> (p. 192)

The absence of a word specifying a place appears here to be the condition of the enigma that will never be solved and, therefore, the condition of the indefinite recurrence of the narrative. While this word, which Claire Lannes admits thinking of (in a no more clumsy and perforated manner than anyone else) belongs to an "I am not", it is in this in this absence – in this hole that is both linguistic (*lalangue*) and spatialised (the Other as place) – that her being, her *parlêtre*, is held. One point of the epic leap thus goes in front of the "I do not think" that is characteristic of the passage to the act. I did not remember, while I was following this thread of *L'Amante anglaise*, that Lacan had traced this path on one of his quadrangular schema: a path – if we may call it this – that we will not follow step by step but dash across in a single leap.[39]

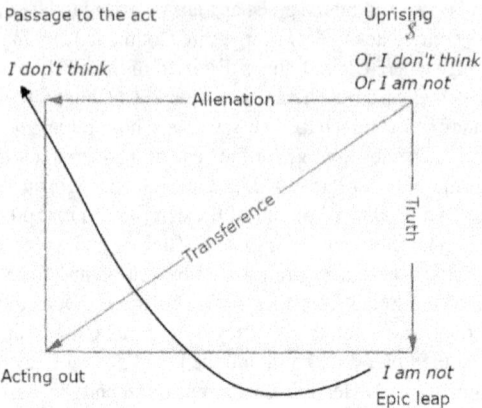

Figure 3.6 Schéma 5.

Here, what Lacan called a "jump" of the subject "to one of the apices of the tetrahedron"⁴⁰ is drawn. Nonetheless, with *L'Amante anglaise*, we find ourselves in the presence – not so much of a progressive displacement of the subject that is fundamentally and immediately barred from the place of "I am not" towards the place of "I do not think" – but rather in the presence of two distinct places, from which the subject splits. Neither of these two positions: "I am not" and "I do not think", are bound. Claire Lannes does not say "the word that would matter": saying this word would, she affirms, make her someone buried alive. We also wonder what, in seeing her maintain her narrative – her "I am not", her epic leap – holds her there in front of a particular and unpassable threshold, as if she is stuck.

Stuck ... In front of what? I shall respond by continuing this reading of *L'Amante anglaise* in the manner that one could have already noted. This reading comes back to one of Lacan's schemas: a reading, therefore, with the story (*avec de l'ecrit*) a largely Lacanian manner of proceeding and maintained by him until the end of the journey. A week before the session of 17 January 1968, from which we extracted Schéma 5, he added to his quadrangular schema rather a large number of indications. Of these, I will retain just two (even though I risk the reproach of having oversimplified it): on the one hand, $-\varphi$, placed where the epic leap has been inscribed; on the other hand, *petit a*, where Lacan situated the passage to the act.

Claire Lannes' fear of herself and her words being buried alive forces her to no longer go on with her narrative in which she is not, to the point of recognising that she is not, "there where $-\varphi$ was." This is what, with Lacan, we called "castration".⁴¹ However, we nonetheless note that the other Lacanian term, *désêtre* (un-being), is remarkably present in her fear. Because this dread is the

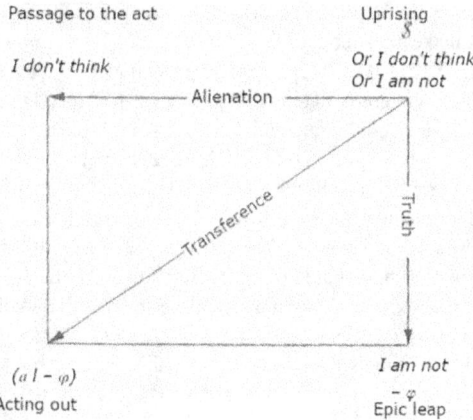

Figure 3.7 Schéma 6.

fear that both a premature and overly invasive presence of death (the first and second death) will prevent her experience of *dèsêtre* (un-being), from being perceived by her as not contravening life.

Now, this limit imposed upon the epic leap responds to another limitation that concerns the passage to the act. Two very different limits because the epic leap connotes, whereas the passage to the act denotes.

An incomplete passage to the act

Any "I think" that forms a narrative can feed the impulse of the passage to the act which instead, is the manifestation of an "I am ...", to be written with suspension points as something like "I am that one who ...", must be specified.

A lot of information could be gathered with regard to what could have pushed one to the act; the pieces of information could even make a narrative, if anyone applied himself to this task. Marie-Thérèse Bousquet came from Cahors as a housekeeper for Claire Lannes: she is Claire's cousin, is of her blood.[42] Marie-Thérèse achieved, without any struggle, her status as mistress of the house: she is at home (p. 107) in Claire's house, a house that Claire has never appropriated. We can therefore deduce that there was no actual rivalry between the two when it came to taking the role of mistress of the house; nor any when it comes to Alfonso, whom Claire likes very much (p. 63) and with whom Marie-Thérèse sleeps from time to time (p. 63) but – it is said – as "a sort of convenience" (p. 72). Another trait is present, also in minor mode: fearing a scandal or a suicide, Marie-Thérèse watches over Claire "kindly" and because "it was necessary".

Marie-Thérèse's condition as a deaf-mute comprises three characteristics. (1) It does not make her unhappy: she is "lively" (p. 147), "strong" and "always content" (p. 137). (2) It does not prevent her from understanding all that is said, by lip-reading, to the point that "nothing escaped her" (p. 84). (3) It makes it unthinkable that one could argue with her (p. 143). These three characteristics aggravate Claire: "I'm telling you that I have a character that cannot tolerate people who eat and sleep well" (p. 148). She knows that, apart from her infirmity, Marie-Thérèse, in contrast to Alfonso, was not "on her side ... If she had been normal, she would have been the queen of the other side" (p. 177).

To think, from all this, that these characteristics were the determining factor in the passage to the act, is an interpretative step that we shall refrain from taking. Numerous indications grasp the passage to the act more closely and arise from a different register entirely. What is this about? About orality: more precisely, a certain oral disgust to which the passage to the act puts an end.

One could have seen this coming if one had taken seriously several initial passages to the act heralding the one that will come last. Yes, because it so happens that certain passages to the act come in series, the first ones carrying the intention of avoiding the occurrence of a passage to the act that is judged as more serious because it is more violent. According to which criteria?[43] The ultimate passage to the act ends by death putting an end to the series.

Pierre Lannes speaks:

> Claire sometimes did stupid things, things that could have been dangerous ... She was destructive, reckless. She burned all the newspapers at once in the fireplace. She broke things, often plates: she threw them into the bin. Or she hid them in secret places, she buried them in the garden ... She cut things up as well.
>
> (p. 110)

With Duras, we can see in these passages to the act so many calls that will never be heard, or so many preparative actions, rough drafts of the act that will partially be a resolution.

It was a matter of "destroying", "burying", "cutting up", "throwing": these verbs will intervene later, as we have seen. In contrast to the equivocal *Niederkommen* of the "young homosexual woman" (in which the S_1 "falling" represents the subject for the S_2 "giving birth"), these terms are not signifiers, but operate as many other signs in the configuration to the passage to the act. Nonetheless, Pierre Lannes' testimony emphasises the plates, to which Claire refers several times. She says:

> At the bottom of the stack of plates, I see the design of the plates bought in Cahors, three days before the marriage ... It begins again. I know that I am going to be carried away into the thoughts of the plates, towards those things. Well, then, I have had enough, do you understand? I want someone

to come and take me away. I desire three or four walls, an iron door, a barred window, and for Claire Lannes to be confined inside there. So, I open the window and break the plates so that someone can hear me and can come to take me away. But suddenly, she is there. She watches me break the plates. She smiles and runs to alert Pierre.

(p. 172)

Because breaking plates is not, after all, that serious (really?), all these acts were (unuttered) appeals to be confined, to be stopped, but because they were not explicit, these appeals were not heard, and as such Claire Lannes did not know how to avoid her ultimate passage to act (but, her preceding passages to the act attest to her having thought about stopping herself). Instead, James Frame just avoided his passage to the act (the murder of his beloved wife) by going to the police commissioner and begging to be taken to the asylum so that he could be kept locked away.[44] Her ultimate passage to the act appeases Claire Lannes. The reason for this is not so much to be seen in the plates, but in their contents, particular contents. Metonymy, if you wish. What contents? The meat in sauce that Marie-Thérèse cooked (p. 136) and that Claire ate without saying how much this food and the very act of eating it horrified her.

Another metonymy intervenes here, according to which the cook is given the least appetising qualities of what she was cooking. One particular day, Claire points to Marie-Thérèse and observes to her husband that she looks like a "little ox" (p. 108). She later makes a point, regarding this expression, of correcting the person who is interrogating her:

"One day, you told him that Marie-Thérèse Bousquet resembled an animal."

"That's not true. I said, 'a little ox'. And from her back. it was true."

(p. 140)

Marie-Thérèse is fat and even "too fat for the house" (p. 150). Claire remarks that she eats a lot and describes her as "an enormous mass of deaf meat" (p. 177). She could no longer tolerate seeing Marie-Thérèse eat (p. 147).

No more meat in sauce ever! The murder of Marie-Thérèse Bousquet ends Claire Lannes' disgust for the meat in sauce[45] that she forced herself to eat in silence. How to finish with it? She vomits it off the parapet of the viaduct. Nothing could be simpler. This time, the passage to the act is expressed in one word: "vomit" (p. 148). One of Lacan's comments clarifies this disgust:

For the human species, sexuality is obsessive – rightly so. It is in effect abnormal in the sense that I defined it: there is no sexual relation. Freud, that is to say a case, took the credit for noticing that neurosis was not structurally obsessional, but hysteric in her foundation: that is to say, linked to the fact that there is no sexual relation, that there people to whom it disgusts, which is a sign, a positive sign, that it makes them vomit.[46] [*Translator's note*: Allouch makes the point that Freud published a few cases, none of which were plausible to generalise something completely different to vignettes, that are supposed to teach how to treat plurals of so-called mental conditions with a general rule applicable to all.]

Taking into account the line above, it appears less strange the butchery that Claire Lannes inflicts on Marie-Thérèse's corpse transforming it, in meat in sauce after the murder. Likewise, some people in mourning have consecutive dreams that offer the bereaved the possibility of having for an instant *present the* deceased before the moment of death, by imagining the person alive. Similarly, the butcher cuts up the meat *before* it is put into sauce.

Can we, however, affirm that Claire Lannes' passage to act coincides with Lacan's description of the passage to the act that he gives when he interrogates, for a second time, the "young homosexual woman"? Letting fall, he put forward, is "the essential correlation to any sudden connection of the subject with what he is as *petit a*."[47] This formula would have been appropriate if Marie-Thérèse Bousquet's corpse had, in its entirety, been meat in sauce. But this was not at all. Claire Lannes treated the body in two different ways. The "I do not think" of the passage to the act finds its limit there, just as the "I am not" of the epic leap has not reached its "I am not $-\varphi$". At the top left of Schéma 4, we read two conjoined indications: "I do not think" that a hyphen separates from "where *petit a* was". Claire Lannes does not carry her "I do not think" to the point "where *petit a* was". It follows that the unfinished passage to the act returns to the epic leap just as, similarly, the unfinished epic leap returned to the passage to the act.

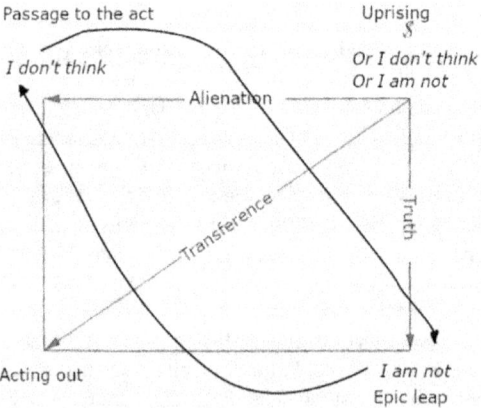

Figure 3.8 Schéma 7.

Christine Papin would have attained the realisation of the passage to the act but somehow in the opposite way of what Claire Lannes was attempting, since her passage to the act does not assimilate her victims to objects of disgust, but rather with appetising oral objects, such as rabbits and bread rolls that are "ready to cook" – the expression with which Mayete Viltard ended the chapter she wrote for La *"Solution" du passage à l'acte*.[48] Where, in passing to the act, Claire Lannes *vomits*, the Papin sisters *eat* (*incorporate*).

Two different re-settings

The epic leap and the passage to the act were, each in its own way, limited, that is, unfinished. On the one hand, the epic leap could not reach the "I am not $-\varphi$" that characterises it and offers proof of its effectiveness. On the other hand, the passage to the act did not take its "I do not think" to the point where it could have reached "where *petit a* was" that would, too, have made it effective. The epic leap and the passage to the act *in fine* came short, which cannot be envisaged if one is not detached from the various feelings that everyone experiences when dealing with such atrocities.

Two traits of the case now find their reason. They are linked, and this unique reason is common to both. Precisely because neither one nor the other fully played its part (so to speak), there had to be two non-achievements. In other words, the "subject at the outset", summoned to choose between "I am not" and "I do not think", was not able to resolve (to both choose and find his solution), inclining towards one or the other choice. This subject is not truly situated either at the top left (passage to the act) or at the bottom right (epic leap) of Schéma 7. What results is a sort of rebound effect, which arises from the above-mentioned reason. This is what Lacan called, as we have seen, a "jump": not the epic leap, but a movement by which the subject reaches one of the apices of the tetrahedron. The subject is bounced, I would say, from one to the other of these apices. The hole constituted in Claire Lannes' narrative by her determined refusal to specify where Marie-Thérèse Bousquet's head is, marks the point of the non-achievement of the epic leap: this non-achievement returns to the passage to the act (see Schéma 4). And the facts that Marie-Thérèse Bousquet's body was not taken in its entirety as meat in sauce and the head was treated quite differently in a mourning ritual, evoked the other jump, in which the aborting of the passage to the act returns the subject to the epic leap. Two re-settings, therefore, in the sense that a certain placing is moved elsewhere. Nonetheless, the passage to the act and the epic leap are not mixed up with each other.

Here, we clearly have a double articulation[49] of the two analytics of sex. The first, where the object (*petit a*) is in play without, however, effectively falling, and where the passage to the act must be situated, and the second, that of the "there is no sexual relation", which is not reached either as we see in the fact that it remains short of reaching $-\varphi$.

Now we notice that the pivot of each of these re-settings is Marie-Thérèse Bousquet's head: the head as not being located for the return of the epic leap to the passage of the act; the head as not being identified as meat in sauce for the return of the passage to the act to the epic leap. Is it only a matter of this head? "A fear of losing her head a bit" possessed Marguerite Duras while she was writing *Le Ravissement de Lol V. Stein*.[50]

Psychoanalysis as practised by Jungians consists of attaching to culture certain phenomena referred to by the patient, which appear to him as both enigmatic and "idiotic, in the first sense of the term, that is, only pertaining to him".[51] This procedure can have a calming effect on the patient (the name given to the analysand among Jungians) by letting him see that he is not as mad as he perhaps thought he was. We qualify this as psychotherapy. Nonetheless, and like Freud who admitted to using the lever of suggestion, we shall not refrain from using it, as Claire Lannes' different treatment of the two parts of Marie-Thérèse Bousquet's body (her head and the pieces of the rest of her corpse) finds its correspondence ... among the Aztecs. They did not treat the heart (object of a cardiectomy) of those they sacrificed in the same way as they treated the other pieces of the corpse, which were eaten by certain chosen ones. Here, too, we have the spiritual, even sacred, dimension: a god is present.[52] This is also made clear in the work, *Du gout de l'autre. Fragments d'un discours cannibale* by Mondher Kilani,[53] which explores the symbolic and metaphorical dimension of cannibalism. In this regard, we recall the necrophagia of the Cynics and Stoics, the manifestation of their contempt for death, and also Montaigne who, in the chapter of his *Essais* devoted to cannibalism, wrote that Chrysippus and Zenon saw nothing wrong with eating human corpses if nothing else was available to eat.

The name "*Amante anglaise*"

The fact that Claire Lannes' "I do not think" does not reach and coincide with the object *petit a* and as *a*, being absorbed by disappearing in it, converges with two main data of the case: the choice of the title (*L'Amante anglaise*) and the treatment reserved for this name which, like the name of God and the name of the agent of Cahors, is not her own name.

Orality is also dominant here: "I thought this: *l'Amante anglaise* is the opposite of meat in sauce" (p. 150). "She wrote *la menthe* ["the mint" – in French, sounds exactly like *l'amante* – the lover] there as *amante*/lover. And *anglaise* ["English" – in French, sounds exactly like *en glaise* – glazed/in clay] as *en glaise*, just the same as 'of earth', 'of sand'" (p. 124). Claire transliterates the syntagma: no longer "*la menthe anglaise*" ("the English mint") but "*l'amante en glaise*" [the lover in glaze/clay]. She eats the plant, which is her favourite: "I ate it sometimes to cleanse myself" (p. 150). In the manner of Claude Lévi-Strauss giving an account of myths, we shall point out that English mint opposes, term by term, meat in sauce. Claire is thin, whereas Marie-Thérèse is fat; she likes fish, whereas Marie-Thérèse cooks meat so much that she becomes meat (p. 89). The mint is a *pharmakon* that can counteract the effect of the eating of meat in sauce – which, Claire says, transforms her into a sewer (*égout*): "I was worse than a sewer [a *ragout*?] before the crime. Now, less and less" (p. 190). But the crime was necessary: no matter how much care she gave the plant by cultivating it in her garden (p. 124), the *pharmakon* was ineffective. It was necessary for her to vomit.

Thus, Marguerite Duras' choice of title appears to take up the intelligence that she describes through a statement made by Claire Lannes: "I was not intelligent enough to speak of the intelligence I had, and of this intelligence, I could not speak" (p. 163). This title allows itself to lie between two possible designations: her name "*menthe anglaise*" and "Claire Lannes", her own name. She could not be "*menthe anglaise*" and defeat the meat in sauce; she could only be Claire Lannes if her interlocutor, finally, were willing to hear her. An in-between, a suspense: the sign of something not accomplished that thus finds itself as much at the level of the epic leap, where Claire Lannes does not reach $-\varphi$, as at the level of the passage to the act, where she does not become the object *a*. If there is a place on Schéma 4 where the name *amante anglaise* can be inscribed, it would be the place towards which the line of the transference is moving, the place where, on some schema and lodged in a single lunula, but separated, are (*petit a*) and ($-\varphi$).

Three limits are presented and are so tightly correlated that we could acknowledge the Borromean nature of their connection as, if one is crossed, the others would also be: (1) the limit of the epic leap, which preserves *petit a*; (2) the limit of the passage to the act that stands without reaching, $-\varphi$; (3) the limit of Claire Lannes' telling, which does not deliver the word that would specify where the head is, the word that would make of her someone buried alive. "If I told you where the head is, would you still speak to me?" (p. 193). Discouraged, her interlocutor – a new and fourth limit – admits defeat and gives up interrogating her any longer.

This moment, which is both final and inconclusive, is also the moment when, confronted by this surrender, Claire Lannes can at last express her demand: "If I were in your place, I would listen. Listen to me" (p. 195). In this, she differs from Christine Papin after her passage to the act. Christine Papin is alive to the point of unobtrusively situating in her place the unknown reason for what happened: "Where is this unknown reason?" she asks. Her interlocutor's response, unreservedly immersed in the psy universe: "In you?" To which she retorts: "Why? Why not in her? Or in the house? In the knife? Or in death? Yes, in death" (p. 169). In the death that did not kill *her*.

Notes

1 This play has been performed many times and was performed recently, in 2017, in Paris at the Théâtre du Lucernaire. The title role was played by Madéline Renaud. An article, by Michèle Ruty, with Madéline Renaud's photograph in the role, was published in *Littoral*, no. 43, entitled "*L'Amante anglaise*: interprétation d'un

crime". [Throughout this chapter, unless otherwise specified the references are to the novel by Marguerite Duras: *L'Amante anglaise* (1967).]
2 Marguerite Duras, *Œuvres complètes*, Vol. I (Paris, Gallimard, "Bibliothèque de la Pléiade", 2011, p. 1263).
3 The conception of a "magic circle" is presented in Jean Allouch, *La Scène lacanienne et son cercle magique* (Paris, Epel, 2018).
4 Marta Mattoni traced the successive intersections of Lacan and Duras. Her unpublished article, "Lol V. Stein entre Duras y Lacan", gathers together all the references relative to the information above.
5 Just as, sometimes, a theft is signed by faeces, left in the place.
6 The quotation from *Le Monde*, as well as the photograph of the intersection of the Montagne Pavée viaduct and the railway line, were republished in an article in the *Bulletin municipal* of Savigny-sur-Orge in June 2009. The article was quite rightly titled "Un crime à Savigny-sur-Orge: le mystère de la tête sans oreilles (1949–1950)" ["A crime at Savigny-sur-Orge: the mystery of the earless head (1949–1950)"].
7 A useful task to do could be titled, "The tic and the passage to the act".
8 Perhaps a representation of Duras herself, just as Hitchcock made brief appearances in some of his films?
9 Please refer to my commentary on this hardness in Jean Allouch, *L'Amour Lacan* (Paris, Epel, 2009, p. 276). There, I discuss the way in which it could be raised. As for knowing what it involves, one could refer to D. H. Lawrence's novel, *Lady Chatterley's Lover* (1932), André Topia's edition, translated by F. Roger-Conaz, Afterword by André Malraux (Paris, Gallimard, "Folio Classique", 1933, p. 358).
10 Homer was the subject of debates that, at the time, brought so much to Nietzsche. See Friedrich Nietzsche, *Le Cas Homère*, edited and prefaced by Carlotta Santini, Afterword by Pierre Judet de la Combe, translated by Guy Fillion and Carlotta Santini (Paris, Éditions de l'EHESS, 2017). Nietzsche called Homer "the quintessence of an aesthetic singularity" (p. 64).
11 I presented this between-effect in *La Scène lacanienne et son cercle magique* (Paris, Epel, 2018).
12 Please refer to Chapter XV of Jean Allouch, *L'Amour Lacan* (Paris, Epel, 2009) to find Lacan's references to this poem and, unexpectedly perhaps, the study of a lapsus made by Lacan when he was quoting it.
13 Lacan even came back to this poem a second time – after 1953, "Fonction et champ ...", in 1972 ("Le savoir du psychanalyse", 6 January 1972). Please see my commentary in Jean Allouch, *L'Amour Lacan* (Paris, Epel, 2009).
14 Jacques Lacan, *...ou pire*, 8 March 1972.
15 A certain connection between the two analytics of sex also follows. This Other/Between [*Autre/Entre*] "in fading, in not existing ... becomes the place where the relation is written". It could not be a matter of the writing of the sexual relation, whereby the "is written" can do no more here than refer to the "formulae of sexuation" (Jacques Lacan, *Encore*, session of 13 March 1973). These formulae envisage the phallus as function, "phallic function", whereas what we are dealing with is its absence in the problematic of the non-existent sexual relation. From this, "displacement" in the quotation above can be read as referring to the passage, to the transformation and to the turning of the absent phallus in the active phallic function. Such a displacement is necessary if one wishes to affirm the non-existence of the sexual relation without, nonetheless, disregarding the fact that sexual acts definitely occur. The lack of phallus in the sexual relation refers to the second analytic of sex whereas, taken as phallic function, the phallus having become function plays a certain part in the first analytic of sex. The same goes for the Other: although non-existent, it is not inactive.

16 George-Henri Melenotte documented the various mentions of *d'entre* by Lacan (*Freud incognito. Danse avec Moïse*, Paris, Epel, 2017, pp. 197–209).
17 Jacques Lacan, "Conférence de presse à Rome", 1974 (*Pas-tout Lacan*, https://ecole-lacanienne.net/bibliolacan/pas-tout-lacan).
18 Note the disparity: "woman" rather than "female", which we would expect after "male".
19 Francis Dupré, *La "Solution" du passage à l'acte. Le double crime des sœurs Papin* (Toulouse, Érès, 1984, available on the Éditions Epel website).
20 Perhaps it is interesting to know the list of contributors to this article: with the exception of Marc Barbut, they were Jean Pouillon, A. J. Greimas, Maurice Godelier, Pierre Pourdieu, Pierre Macherey and Jacques Ehrmann. A dash of contempt made Lacan say, "In short, there's not much in this article."
21 The Klein group is mentioned in "*La Logique du fantasme*", a written account of the seminar of 1966–1967 (Jacques Lacan, *Autres écrits*, Paris, Éditions du Seuil, 2001, pp. 323–328) without any clear mention of Lacan's use of it, and with barely any concern for the logic of this group, except for the discreet indication (24 January 1968) that his schematics were apparently "of the Klein group kind".
22 François Balmès, *Structure, logique, aliénation. Recherches en psychanalyse* (Toulouse, Érès, 2011, pp. 103–126, the chapter entitled "Le quadrangle").
23 François Balmès, *Structure, logique, aliénation. Recherches en psychanalyse* (Toulouse, Érès, 2011, p. 130). Balmès also writes (on the same page) that Lacan's use of the Klein group's structure consists of *bricolage*. The primacy of content over form prohibits all formalised use, all blind calculations" – which is true to a large extent, but not absolutely.
24 Lacan's writing of the four discourses, which also includes four terms and four places, has sometimes resulted in a presentation that recalls the presentation of the schemas of the *vel of alienation* (in the seminars of 17 June 1970 or 17 March 1971). We cannot admit, any more than we can declare, that this resemblance is "fortuitous", that the connections established in each case between the terms refer to the same formal constraints. It is also amusing to note that the barred subject $\$$, lodged high up on the right of the schemas of the *vel* of alienation, finds the same place in the analyst's discourse.
25 Jacques Lacan, Seminar *L'Acte psychanalytique*, session 17 January 1968. The schemas represented here came from the remarkable critical version of his seminar, accessible on the L'École lacanienne website.
26 Jean Allouch, *La Scène lacanienne et son cercle magique: Des fous se soulèvent* (Paris, Epel, 2017).
27 The same goes for the choice, "Your money or your life?", widely discussed by Lacan. However, these two alternatives are not identical.
28 "There is, in effect, a correspondence between alienation as the inevitable choice of *I do not think* and repetition as the inevitable choice of the passage to the act. Indeed, the other term that is impossible to choose is the acting-out correlative of *I am not*" (Seminar *L'Acte psychanalytique*, session 28 February 1968).
29 Here, I am concurring with the reading of François Balmès, according to which the corollary of the choice "I am not" is "I think" whereas, inversely, the corollary of "I do not think" is "I am".
30 Refer to the first chapter of *La Scène lacanienne et son cercle magique* (Paris, Epel, 2018).
31 He is her uncle, her mother's youngest brother and is the same age as her (p. 93). "They knew each other since childhood" (p. 117).
32 Cited by Jacques Lacan, *De la psychose paranoïaque dans ses rapports avec la personnalité* (1932) (Paris, Éditions du Seuil, 1975, pp. 183–184).
33 Text written by Marguerite Duras for a production of *Le Théâtre de l'Amante anglaise*, mise-en-scène by Ahmed Madani (theatre-contemporain.net).

34 Marguerite Duras, *Œuvres complètes*, Vol. I (Paris, Gallimard, "Bibliothèque de la Pléiade", 2011, p. 1574 (notice)).
35 In the usual sense of the term.
36 Classical: many lovers who have been separated, often for a long time, experience the need to see each other one more time, without either of them expecting anything from the other.
37 Subjected to the scent of such thoughts, it is better to behave like a Chinese monkey (some advice on technique).
38 Could the Durassian production, as extended and varied as it may be, be a letter addressed to God? Would we still be interested in this only because the question of what took place between her and God remains pertinent? The name "Donnadieu" allows us to hear three things: a "gift to God" [*un don* – a gift, *à Dieu* – to God]; and also "Dona Dieu" [*Dona* – woman], the wife or mistress of God; or the "femme-Dieu", the female God [*femme* – female; *Dieu* – God]. What could she do, other than write under a different name, when God is dead or, even better, unconscious (Lacan)? And this without, nonetheless, cutting the link between the two names that are joined by a thread: the first letter ["D"], which is also the first letter of the name of *Dieu* [God]. Here we find the echo of the discreet but decisive presence of God, which we noted with regard to Louis Althusser (see Chapter II, pp. 67–68 of the original and pp. 000–000 of this translation).
39 Jacques Lacan, Seminar *L'Acte psychanalytique,* session 17 January 1968 (critical version, schematics reconstructed from the notes taken by the audience). The International Lacanian Association's [ALI] transcription also refers to the drawing of this leap [two different sources of Lacan's seminar].
40 Jacques Lacan, Seminar *L'Acte psychanalytique*, session 17 January 1968.
41 One could be quite rightly surprised by this manner of castration that seems so different from, and even opposed to, one's general understanding of the term.
42 Alfred Bousquet, her father, is the eighth brother of her mother, Adeline Bousquet (pp. 146–147).
43 It's a good bet that, in the implicit and uncertain reference to a continuum of violence of increasingly great intensity, death has the highest ground. Here, the modern prejudice intervenes, at least in the West, and since God was proclaimed dead, according to which being alive is the most precious thing ever. This is not so: among other things, the passage to the act and the epic leap are testament to this.
44 James Frame, *Philosophie de la folie* (1860), edited and translated from English by David Allen (Paris, Epel, 2018).
45 Blood is sometimes used in the making of such sauce. Not long before her murder, Claire Lannes had noticed a smear of blood on Marie-Thérèse Bousquet's neck, something she could see because the latter had changed her hair style.
46 Jacques Lacan, *L'insu que sait de l'une-bévue s'aile à mourre*, session of 19 April 1977. [*Translator's note*: There are different possible translations for this seminar, but I leave the choice to the reader.]
47 Jacques Lacan, *L'Angoise*, 23 January 1963. I discussed this statement in *Ombre de ton chien. Discours psychanalytique, discours lesbian* (Paris, Epel, 2004).
48 Francis Dupré, *La "Solution" du passage à l'acte. Le double crime des sœurs Papin* (Toulouse, Érès, 1984, available on the Éditions Epel website).
49 Syntagma, but not in the sense that some linguists attribute to the term.
50 Marguerite Duras, *Œuvres complètes*, Vol. II (Paris, Gallimard, 2011, p. 1684).
51 *Idiotês* in Greek: "simple, particular", as opposed to the magistrate, the public official, the specialist. Passing through classical Latin ("ignorant"), the term increasingly took on the pejorative meaning that it now has: "imbecile, moron". Throughout the centuries, university discourse constituted itself in always devaluing this repellent figure. Its (*objet a*)?

52 Would this be true of Philippe Sollers, an amateur of crime documentaries that present murderers who cut the bodies of their victims into pieces? See Philippe Sollers, *Centre* (Paris, Gallimard, 2018, pp. 65–66). With regard to the erotic dimension of cannibalism, one can refer to p. 130 of *Moi et lui* by Alberto Moravia (Paris, Flammarion, 1971), in which a woman recounts scenario which, intensifying her masturbatory act, takes her to orgasm. We cannot mention this novel without indicating that it questions what has been constructed under the name sublimation: the phallus is the objection of conscience made to sublimation.
53 Mondher Kilani, *Du gout de l'autre. Fragments d'un discours cannibale* (Paris, Éditions du Seuil, 2018).

Conclusion
Enlightened passage to the act: Jacques Lacan

Another relevance of the passage to the act in psychoanalysis, which has been neglected so far, will allow (among other things) an appreciation of the impassable abyss that separates the way in which the passage to the act is envisaged within the International Psychoanalytical Association (the IPA) from the way it is envisaged by Jacques Lacan in his description of what happens at the end of an analytical journey, an end described as "an enlightened passage to the act". This is an opportune occasion to commend Jacques Derrida who stated, in 2000, that the word "psychoanalysis" should henceforth only be in the plural form. If any doubt remains about the fact that Lacan, with S.I.R. [the three registers, Symbolic, Imaginary, Real], introduced a new paradigm into the Freudian field, one could only – having noticed this abyss – admit that doubt has been erased.

The IPA, or how to anticipate what one wishes to avoid

In 2006, Louise de Urtebey, a doctor of psychopathology and training analyst of the Paris Psychoanalytical Society, published a work entitled *Si l'analyste passe à l'acte*[1] ("If the analyst passes to the act"). [*Translator's note*: Please note that the references for quotations from de Urtebey's book may not be exact.] With reason, she remarks that, while it is known about by some (the protagonists, their entourage, the psychoanalytical association), the psychoanalyst's "passage to the sexual act" (her main theme, her question) is silenced most of the time ... except for certain cases that have caused a scandal. Her book puts an end to this silence: not through the detailed study of several cases (there are only clinical vignettes), but through the theoretical exploration of the problem.[2] We could have therefore qualified this work as courageous if de Urtebey had dispensed with moral considerations under the guise of psychoanalytical theory, and if her work were not – as it has been described – "a warning".[3] It is not at all a warning, and this work therefore deserves our interest.

DOI: 10.4324/9781003504092-5

Conclusion

The problem of the psychoanalyst's passage to the act was made more evident and obvious in a turning point of psychoanalytical practice largely shared within the IPA, and Louise de Urtebey indicates this. Until the end of the 1950s, "former classical theories about the counter-transference" were held: theories that restated the Freudian position inviting the psychoanalyst to be the master or, according to Freud, "*indifferenz*", of the situation,[4] in order to maintain "the objectivity and exactitude" of the science of psychoanalysis (p. 93). There is no doubt that this position was found to be untenable. The countertransference, from then onwards, was no longer "an enemy to be beaten but rather … a mirror of the transference and a means of understanding the analytical situation" (p. 94).[5] Psychoanalytical psychology has gone from uni-personal to bi-personal (p. 40, so much so that the existence of the *conjoint* analyst-patient fantasm" (p. 47, emphasis mine) is affirmed without blinking, as is the fantasm of "a *meeting* point previously repressed in the two egos" (p. 69, emphasis mine). The term "couple" is used regularly by de Urtebey who sees nothing odd in stating that the patient and analyst form a couple: from this, it follows that psychoanalysis mutates into couple therapy. There floats the scent of the sexual relation, which can also be recognised in the "*catastrophic* fact, constructed by two, of the transference and countertransference meeting each other, to accept, to jouir, and to suffer" (p. 105, de Urtebey's italics)

This change regarding the countertransference opened a Pandora's box. Thus, together with Lucy Tower, we saw the candour and open-mindedness of concluding that "erotic responses troubled nearly all analysts" (p. 12). As a reaction to this change, one would "strive through the countertransference to become the good parent" who was lacking in the patient's childhood (p. 61). Another would consider that a psychoanalysis cannot be terminated if the analyst has not been able to "fantasise erotically and lovingly" about his patient (p. 68), to have loved and desired the patient at the oedipal genital stage (p. 90). Someone else would find it sometimes appropriate to communicate to the patient what the latter has made him endure (p. 96). Going even further in this vein, some would practise self-revelation by speaking to their patients about themselves (p. 96). Others would make reference to their erotic countertransference, which, according to the author, is the establishment of a *folie à deux*[6] (p. 97).

We have just looked over some of the psychoanalytical positions and practices that came out of this Pandora's box, the opening of which has demanded more than a counterpart. Brought into the open air, the countertransference can only avoid being pushed to the point of the passage to "the transgressive sexual act" by having recourse to its analysis. Two patients are then present in the analytical scene and two analyses are necessary: one for the actual patient and one for the psychoanalyst seized in his countertransference and no longer having, as Freud wished, "a thick skin" (p. 88). Having acknowledged the countertransference, "the analyst is himself *the second patient* and must self-analyse himself" (p. 24).

However, the analysis of the countertransference, while judged to be crucial, is not sufficient to guarantee that there will be no passage to the act. The analyst has to be also the "keeper of the setting" and thus respect it himself. In this regard, de Urtebey distinguishes both large and small deviations. We smile on learning that it is not too serious if the analytical session begins or extends by a minute or two before or after the agreed time, while ten minutes before or after is viewed as a passage to the act of the psychoanalyst (pp. 53–54).[7] A great number of rules specify the setting, which is sometimes the object of a contract between the psychoanalyst and the patient: consistency of the sessions' durations; sessions starting and ending at the agreed time; no physical contact; the two alone in the consulting room; fees paid promptly; the initiation of speech reserved for the patient; professional confidentiality; no moral or aesthetic judgement on the analyst's part; no taking advantage of the patient's regression; relative anonymity of the psychoanalyst as a person; no denying of the hate in the analyst; no taking sides with or against the patient. Yet another rule, "the prohibition of the passage to the act for the analyst" (p. 24), is elevated to the rank of *ground rule* (de Urtebey's emphasis) as its "transgression" puts an end to the analysis. This, as we shall demonstrate, highlights what is at play in the establishment of, and respect for, the setting. One does not know why, for example, loving an analysand would be less grave than having a relationship with him or her (p. 100). Does love do less damage than sex?

So, what is expected of such a setting? It facilitates "the analyst's capacity to survive the attacks of the patient" (p. 22); it opposes the efforts of non-neurotic patients "to establish a setting other than the analyst's" (p. 22); it is a container (p. 30); it is what the passage to the act crosses and attacks (p. 51), hence the terms "transgression" and even "violation"; it maintains the Hippocratic oath (p. 65); it is "intended to allow the patient to pour his heart out in safety" (p. 98).[8] Who cannot but notice that the rules configuring the setting and the functions attributed to the setting are at the service of the pleasure principle: in other words, to keep the minimum of excitation? That it is all about a buffer that is expected to subdue certain untimely moments of the process?[9] Is this not an attempt to leave outside the field of analysis the very stuff that presents itself for treatment? This is ratified by the author's idea that what must be played out in analysis is of the order of "as if": a "characteristic" that she says is "indispensable in the analytical space" (p. 108): in short, nothing real. In contrast to Freud, de Urtebey denies that transference love is a true love.[10]

The respect for the setting, which is supposed to prevent the sexual passage to the act, isn't it instead what pushes to pass to the act? And so, we can conclude that *the psychoanalyst's passage to the sexual act is the exact manifestation of what the rigid, heavy setting attempted to keep out of the field.* The analyst who passes to "the transgressive sexual act" is one who, more than many others, remains focused on the said "setting". The thesis of de Urtebey's work thus allows itself to be turned over as easily as a crêpe. Thought of as a safeguard, the setting appears as a provocation. The setting ... becomes a *set-up*. And the message of de Urtebey's book, *Si l'analyste passe à l'acte*, which the psychoanalysts of that strand of the IPA share among themselves, is somewhat deploringly expressed: "We cannot provide a setting for those patients who come to us asking for help." In effect, madness would not be madness if it did not break the setting(s) in multiple ways.

Here, perhaps, we can see what motivates Louise de Urtebey's addressing to such an extent the psychoanalyst's passage to the act: her own, unbeknownst, malaise regarding the setting promoted by the group to which she belongs. Was it not the fear of the passage to the act that led to the defining and establishment of this framework? Not long before concluding, de Urtebey writes: "The analyst, weary of his work, disappointed, imprisoned in his consulting room, may experience desires for freedom, for revolt against the Freudian rules, and imagine that an Oedipal sexual activity will liberate him" (p. 175).

A desire for freedom in someone who, for years and years, has believed that he had to burden his shoulders with the yoke of the setting? This conjecture does not seem so out of place when is evaluated against the answer that de Urtebey's book provides to the following question: what must the psychoanalyst do in order to always be self-analysing his countertransference and to always ensure that the setting is respected? He must, we read, have internalised the ethical rules "derived from the identification, notably in the superego and the ideal ego, with the proper father representing the law, with the former analyst, with the masters, with Freud, and with other parental figures of the superego or figures introjected and established in the ideal ego" (p. 20)[11]. It is difficult to imagine that, afflicted by such a superego, an analyst could exercise his/her own freedom in playing the game of the transference of the analysand who does not always expect him to be the person that the setting demands him to be.

The version of the passage to the act conveyed by *Si l'analyste passe à l'acte* is also remarkable in that, in many points, it coincides with the version that we studied while reading the dossier, "*Passer à l'acte*", published by *La Clinique lacanienne*. Here, a false start is immediately made when it is said that Freud's article, "Remembering, repeating and working-through" (published in 1914), was "foundational" to the notion of the passage to the act [pp. 34–36 and p. 82). This is incorrect. There is no "passage to the act" anywhere in Freud. This kind of forcing was made possible by what de Urtebey signals in the clearest manner: she will not use the expression "passage to the act" in the accepted psychiatric sense of the term (p. 51).[12] As we noted, the same abstention characterises "*Passer à l'acte*" (published by *La Clinique lacanienne*). Just as in this work, the passage to the act, for want of being located, comes to designate any act whatsoever in de Urtebey's work. Thus on the part of the patient: not paying for his session; not arriving; being late, etc.; on the part of the psychoanalyst: dozing off in a session (p. 46); allowing the session to go on beyond the agreed time limit (p. 53); seeing a patient who arrives at his usual time but on the wrong day (p. 59), etc. Putting the "psychiatric" passage to the act back into the Freudian *agieren* (the 1914 article) allows us to think of the passage to the act as an act of passage of a symbolic element that could not embark on the right path – the path of speech.

A classified advertisement for a public auction could read: "Primacy of the symbolic not dead!". It is the same among the contributors to *La Clinique lacanienne* as it is for de Urtebey: she writes, for example, that the analytical relation is such that "everything occurs '*as if*', symbolically" (p. 20). Or, furthermore, that the loss of "*as if*" is "connected to an incapacity to symbolise resulting from a serious pathology in the analyst" (p. 108). The equivalence of "*as if*" and "symbolic" does not seem to raise any question at all. Where would "*as if*" be, then, when Freud deciphers a dream by envisaging it as a rebus?

We have endeavoured, here, to climb the slope that both the dossier "*Passer à l'acte*" of *La Clinique lacanienne* and Louise de Urtebey have tumbled down. As a result, the point of falling is no less than the abandonment of the passage to the act. For our endeavour, three criteria were put into play. (1) Criterion of meaning: an action that easily takes place in a narrative cannot be envisaged in the same way as an action that remains utterly enigmatic. (2) The second criterion, which redoubles the first, is of a clinical order: Fethi Benslama brought to light what he called the "epic leap" and the question that the passage to the act cannot be envisaged if this is disregarded. (3) The third criterion also involves a choice, this time of the theoretical order: we chose the *vel* of alienation in order to situate and address both the passage to the act and the epic leap. Consequently, nothing that we could have read here would be valid if any one of these three criteria is rejected.

The application of these criteria has given rise to a surprising, unexpected, datum, both at the moment of writing these pages and, perhaps, when reading them. Through the analysis of Louis Althusser's passage to the act (Chapter II) and even more with Claire Lannes' passage to the act (Chapter III), it appears that these murderous actions come within the realm of the passage to the act, certainly, *but also* within the realm of the epic leap. In this, they differ from the act of the jihadists (paradigm of the epic leap) and the crime of the Papin sisters (exemplary of the passage to the act).

This surprise could give place to a critical re-examination of the passages to the act mentioned previously: the passages to the act of, among others, the "young female homosexual", Marguerite Anzieu, Iris Cabezudo and Ernst Wagner. We could also revisit the famous case of "the man craving fresh brains" and ask whether, rather than an acting-out, it was a passage to the act or an epic leap. We admit that, while we gave it its place, we have not addressed acting-out as we ought have, as the different schemas, which we have presented and which displayed the *vel* of alienation, include – apart from their point of departure – not two but three apices where the *passage to the act*, *acting-out* and *the epic leap* take place. We skipped over acting-out, which was made possible because it occupies a kind of median position between the passage to the act and the epic leap. Nonetheless, this regrettable omission has not impeded what will follow, which concerns the articulation of the passage to the act and the epic leap at the beginning and end of the analytical experience.

The distinction between the passage to the act and the epic leap – the former made from "I do not think" and the latter from "I am not" – intersects the other distinction that I have recently brought to light: the distinction between the two analytics of sex in Lacan. The reading of *L'Amante anglaise* confirmed that the passage to the act arises from the first analytic of sex (the *object a*, on this occasion the oral object), while the second (that of there is no sexual relation) could be assigned to the epic leap (on this occasion, the sending of the love letter and the mourning ritual).

Epic leap and enlightened passage to the act at the end of analysis

The passage to the act/epic leap distinction could also shed some light on the analytic act and the conception of what could be an end of an analysis. This is all the more so because we find in Lacan, beginning in 1967,[13] not only one but at least two, if not three,[14] versions of this end. The conception of how an analysis is ended is common to all three. Nonetheless, this completion was envisaged by Lacan from two different perspectives. Sometimes: as separation of the *a* from *A*, the analyst being discarded, rejected like a waste product[15] (in which case this end could and should be qualified as a passage to the act). Other times: as another manner of separation, which marks each of those at play differently – the analyst as being struck by his/her *unbeing* (*désêtre*) ... and the corresponding subjective destitution of the analysand (in which case, the end should be seen as an epic leap). The first version concerns a particular path of the pulsion and the fantasm ($ <> a$) The second version cannot do so, as it is a matter of a different kind of separation, which concerns the analyst as such and the analysand as such. We should, therefore, recognise the passage to the act in the first version, and an epic leap in the second. Now it is time to affirm, indeed, to refine, this conjecture.

We are all the more invited to do this because Lacan assigned to the analyst the position of "I do not think" that is, as we have said, characteristic of the passage to the act. At first, this appears to contradict what we have said so far: that is, to conceive the end of an analysis as an epic leap, because the very movement of an analysis always highlights what happens *between* the analyst and the analysand. This becomes particularly intense: it is nothing other than the transference, which is found to be – as we know all too well – the place where many analyses do not reach their true ending (we only have to consider Lacan's analyses of Didier Anzieu and Marie de la Trinité,[16] or analyses that had no other ending than the death of the analyst).[17]

Situating the analyst in the (untenable?) position of "I do not think" arises from, according to Lacan, a position of the analyst put into the service of an analysand's journey, which is thought of as "a logic that strangely begins from the alienating choice that is offered between 'I do not think' and 'I am not'".[18] Lacan qualified as "informed" a subject who has reached this point, which is thus demonstrated as a point where the possibility of "what cannot be called anything other than the enlightened – we shall say – passage to the act".[19] So, here, the question of the termination of an analysis is presented as no longer having only two endings but rather, it initially seems, as having three: *passage to the act*, *epic leap* and *enlightened passage to the act*.

First of all, we have the passage to the act of the analyst who adheres to not thinking: a nonetheless strange passage to the act as, far from being a single event, it remains at work throughout the analysis. The affirmation of "I do not think" as the position where the analyst is placed (which, no doubt, arises from an ascesis), plunges Lacan into a difficulty similar to the one he confronted with his "there is no sexual relation";

> as a psychoanalyst, I cannot say this. Look, he said with humour, at the effect that this could have on my clientele! This is also what traps me in the position of *I do not think*.

He cannot say it, and yet ... he does. Thus, he refers to his predicament – a trait whereby we recognise his seriousness. A statement, written rather than transcribed, drives the point home:

> In psychoanalysis, the psychoanalyst is not a subject and in situating his act from the ideal topology of the *object a*, one deduces that by not thinking he operates.[20]

We could wonder if this position of the analyst dispensing with thinking is not simply something unprecedented that the West has created over centuries of philosophy, spirituality and therapeutics. Lacan noticed this, going as far as to conclude that analysis could well disappear and later be seen as merely an "episode" in the history of humanity ... we think of Port-Royal.

> Analysis is – call it what you will – that original experience or artefact or something that perhaps will appear in history not at a certain moment but as some kind of episode, a very legitimate way of dealing with extremely

particular cases, of a practice that was found by chance to open a completely different mode of relations enacted between human beings.[21]

Exempt from eternity, analysis will thus mark its difference from unsinkable Christianism. Who could doubt, therefore, that there is a relation to death that is better configured?

What effect does the absence of thinking in the analyst have on the analysand? We can see it in the analysand being always pushed to accomplish an epic leap and thus bring his analysis to an end. While this affirmation is my own, it is supported by a number of remarks made by Lacan and takes place in the thread of modification previously made to Schéma 3 (Chapter III). While they coexist from the perspective of structure, the three vectors named "*alienation*", "*transference*" and "*truth*" nonetheless draw a subjective path that ends up at the truth. A little imagination will allow the Schéma to be envisaged like the drawing of an open fan, held in the hand at ($). The hand closes the fan: the horizontal line of alienation comes to first join the oblique line of the transference that, now, covers it (passage, if you will, of neurosis to the neurosis of transference); both lines then go behind the vertical line of the truth. The fan is closed. Having started at the choice of "I do not think" (free association, made possible by a passage to the act), the journey comes to an end with "I am not". This truth was, in its time, put under the banner of a "subjective destitution". Once the analysand reaches this point, marked as $-\varphi$, it is then by means of an epic leap that he separates himself from his analyst. Claire Lannes' epic leap could not reach $-\varphi$; she could not know the pleasure of castration. In the end, she demands that someone listen to her – someone who is going to shy away. After her passage to the act, Christine Papin no longer has anything to ask of anyone, not even presidential pardon: she lets herself die.

The "enlightened passage to the act" should now be situated. What is it? To know this, we refer to Schéma 5 – precisely to the curved line that transcribes the subjective movement: the leap from "I am not" to "I do not think".

> It is the subject who has effectuated the task at the end of which he is realised as subject in castration, *qua* lacking in the *jouissance* of the sexual union. It is this that we have to see – by a rotation or a swivel of a certain number of degrees as drawn by this figure here, at 180° – passing or coming back to the point of departure. When he is realised here, precisely here, as I have already emphasised, that the subject who comes here (above left) knows what belongs to the subjective experience and that this experience also implies, if I may say so, that on the left remains what has become of the one whose act is responsible for the path taken: in other words, that for the analyst as we see him now surging up to the level of his act; there is already knowledge of the un-being [*désêtre*] of the subject supposed to know, inasmuch as it is, from this logic, the necessary point of departure.[22]

If we pay some attention to this quotation, it will be clearer than it initially seems. We will focus on two remarks. The first is: if any doubts remained about the fact that an analysis concludes on the register of the second analytic of sex where the non-existence of the sexual relation, the Other (*l'Autresexe*) and the *jouissance* of the Other are at play, these doubts are now put to rest. For, defined as "lacking in the *jouissance* of the sexual union", castration does not intersect nor even rejoint, but is in itself another way of expressing the non-existence of the sexual relation. Lacan:

> The fact that the axiology of psychoanalytic practice proves to be reduced to the sexual, does not contribute to the subversion of ethic that takes place in the inaugural act in which *the sexual is showed by negativities of structure* [emphasis mine].[23]

Here, the meaning of "sexual" in "sexual relation" is specified. There is "no sexual relation" and "castration": are the same. "The subject who has effectuated the task at the end of which he is realised as subject in the castration" has thus attained his "I am not". As this place is the place of the epic leap, we can then conclude that, castrated, it is by means of an epic leap that he puts an end to his analysis. This ending is both radical and not without consequence. "Radical" because there is no question of another "instalment". As Freud said, "The proverb, 'The lion only leaps once', is necessarily correct",[24] and this is "a lion's leap". "Not without consequence" because we have to see this subject "*passing* or returning to the point of departure" (emphasis mine). Here, Lacan is supposing that at the outset, the subject made the choice of "I do not think" – which conforms, moreover, with the rule of free association that is his system of speaking once he begins an analysis. ("It's just come to mind to say ..." is quite a different account to "I think that ...".) It is by means of a passage to the act that he enters into analysis; in other words, that the transference/acting-out is established and (this is the reason that authorises the affirmation that analysis is an experience that ends) it is by means of an enlightened passage to the act that he comes to occupy the place of the analyst after the separation of the analysand and the analyst has happened: the separation that has the status of an epic leap. This is the passage represented by the curved line in Schéma 5.

Moreover, in a word, the enlightened passage to the act was called in another place, "the pass", pass that is thus envisaged at an angle that is essential to it – that of the act. As we can see it is not about a supplemental analysis; or about reconnection with a so-called "unanalysed" aspect (as has been said so often ... and even sometimes practised). The one who passes thus comes to occupy the place of the analyst (without, however, being bound to practise): the place where the rather specific example of the passage to the act can be held, which consists – as this is its definition – of not thinking at all.

Conclusion 79

The enlightened passage to the act is the essence of the passage to the act. Nonetheless, the one who passes does not come back to this place in the same state as when he left it by undertaking an analysis. He comes back to it "enlightened" or even "informed": two terms that can be seen here as equivalent. This will be verified in the quotation below, in which the first reference to the enlightened passage to the act is made (I regret the detours in it, but we have no choice):

> Indeed, if anything pertaining to knowing always leaves a residue, a residue somehow constitutive of its status ... the first question that must be asked – is not – about the partner, of the one who is there, I say as an instrument rather than as an aid, in order for something to operate, something that is the psychoanalysing task at the end of which the subject, let us say it, is informed of the constitutive division after which something opens for him, which we cannot call anything differently or other than passage to the act: shall we say, enlightened passage to the act. It is precisely about knowledge that in every act there is something that as a subject escapes him, that will come to have an effect, and that at the end of his act the realisation is for the moment at least veiled in what is of the act, that should be accomplished as being his own realisation.[25]

A week later, Lacan was more precise about this subject who is "informed" while also manifesting a limit to his own knowing:

> To conceive of what this informed subject should be, we do not have as yet any existing type. (This informed subject) is only discernible with regard to an act that is to be constructed like the one where, reiterating itself, castration establishes itself as passage to the act.[26]

These words express differently what we have already noted: that is, the leap that passes the "I am not" (epic leap) to "I do not think" (passage to the act). They do more, however, in affirming that castration "establishes" the enlightened passage to the act of a henceforth informed subject. This is a post-castration passage to the act: something never seen, imagined or thought.

Without being at all moderate, such Lacanian audacity confronts its own limit, or better say digs a hole, when Lacan admits that "we do not have any existing type" of this informed subject. Let us recall the text "*Proposition d'octobre 1967 sur la psychanalyste de l'école*", dated six months before the words quoted above, we may agree that it was only by having his proposition in mind that Lacan could go so far as to conceive of the possibility of an informed subject like this one, while at the same time stating that none existed before this. He was expecting proof of such a subject's existence from an experience, the experience of *the pass*, recognising thereby that this subject was not within the reach of his analytic practice or of his seminar. Nonetheless, he did not take care that his own demand regarding the pass could run counter to its effective application.[27] It could have been possible if after having proposed it, he had dispensed with any demand concerning it. The fact that he could not was one of the components that he recognised as a failure "of *this* pass".[28]

If, in an inverse movement, we refer to a few years later, specifically 2 November 1973,[29] we may read, in a striking speech by Lacan, that a flash of lightning occurs in the "moment (of the pass) when one decides (here is the will again) either to leave or to enter into the analytic discourse". The notion of the enlightened passage to the act therefore rebounds in the lightning flash of the pass and thus sees itself supported, if not confirmed.

A psychoanalyst, then, is invited to exercise his office by not thinking.[30] Linking the said psychoanalyst to *L'Amante anglaise*, this statement can be expressed in different words: without thoughts and therefore without thinking, the analyst is just anyone. Claire Lannes: "I could have written letters about him, but to whom? … It would have been necessary to send them to just anyone. But just anyone is not easy to find."

Notes

1 Louise de Urtebey, *Si l'analyste passe à l'acte*, preface by Claude Le Guen (Presses universitaires de France, 2006). In this work, the quotations are almost never precisely referenced.
2 Some cases of "transgressive" analysts are referred to: Carl Gustav Jung, Sándor Ferenczi, Ernst Jones and Masud Khan – this latter, she remarks, only committed certain transgressive sexual acts after the death of Donald W. Winnicott, his last psychoanalyst, who thus would be partly responsible for these acts (pp. 153–156). Mention is also made (p. 11) of statistics, documented in the United States and Canada, of 5–20 per cent of passages to the sexual act in "psych" professions. The author also refers to about 20 similar cases that she knew of during her 40 years of psychoanalytic practice (p. 74).
3 The last lines of the work (p. 180) have the reach of a Freudian [*Verneinung*] denegation: "For me, it is not a question of denouncing anyone …", whereas, four lines later, this "anyone" is described as "a black sheep".
4 This *indifferenz* went from hand to hand, from Freud to, now, de Urtebey, passed on by two psychoanalysts, Steven Levy and Lawrence Inderbitzen who, she says (p. 26), remark that Freud does not speak of neutrality. This is, indeed, the problem. The concern of indifference is the concern of the man of power. When he was asked about the most important quality that he believed a president of the Republic should have, François Mitterand replied, "Indifference."
5 Nothing in the work supports the idea of the countertransference being configured as a mirror of the transference (even though the term recurs several times).
6 This is a misunderstanding: the author here does not seem to have the slightest idea of what has been called "*folie à deux*" (see "L'assertitude paranoïaque", *Littoral* (no. 3/4, Paris, Epel, 1982), freely accessible on the Epel website). This misunderstanding is not surprising as the author has indicated that she has treated neurotics and "very few psychotics" (p. 73). Demonstrating a remarkable frankness, she mentions several cases in her practice when she got rid certain patients because the situation with them had reached an impasse.

Conclusion 81

7 Here, we can mention the remark of an eminent member of the IPA (Maurice Bouvet?): when his patient let him know that he was ill and could not attend his session, he said that he would not charge him if his fever went above 38.5 degrees.

8 This is someone who wishes to undertake a training psychoanalysis. First appointment with a training analyst of the International Psychoanalytic association, to whom he expressed his request. Response: "First, calmly undertake your personal analysis and, after that, we shall see." The candidate, whose request was serious, never returns to this person, who pointed out that an analysis could be accomplished in complete calmness.

9 I have come to recognise that these moments "of crisis" are among the most decisive moments in the analytical journey. Two traits demonstrate this: (1) the analysis is on the edge of being interrupted (which happens sometimes); (2) the psychoanalyst is tempted to shift the patient to a colleague or to a psychiatrist. The analysis proves to come close to pharmaceutical medicine, which sees in the crisis both an aggravation of the illness and a possibility of the patient's recovery. In the "dynamic of transference", Freud wrote, "no one can be killed *in abstentia* or *in effigie*". This statement is often quoted. Note that it excludes the phrase "as if".

10 A difficulty here does not seem to have been noticed. If love in analysis is an "as if" love and not a true love – the reason being that it is a renewal of a childhood love – what makes any love in "true life" itself anything other than an "as if" love?

11 The loathing for Lacan, perceptible in this work in a few discreet, numbered indices, no doubt allowed the author to dispense with any discussion of his critique of the end of the analytical journey as an identification with the analyst.

12 This opens the possibility of stating (p. 112) that "the passage to the act is a 'conjoint' creation".

13 See Lacan's "Proposition du 9 octobre 1967 sur le psychanalyste de l'École", page 14, Scilicet 1, (Paris, Éditions du Seuil, 1968). Revue paraissant au Champ freudien, collection dirigée par Jacques Lacan.

The volumes run from number 1 to volume 6/7(double) in 1976 the last one.

14 See José Attal, *La passe à plus d'un titre. La troisième proposition d'octobre de Jacques Lacan* (Paris, L'Unebévue éditeur, 2012). Also, Jean Allouch, *Pourquoi y a-t-il de l'excitation sexuelle plutôt que rien?* (Paris, Epel, 2017, p. 16).

15 Among other possibilities and, in reference to Claire Lannes. Vomited?

16 Marie de la Trinité, *De l'angoisse à la paix* (Paris, Arfuyen, 2006). See more references in Jean Allouch, *L'Amour Lacan* (Paris, Epel, 2009, p. 455, note 21).

17 An unexplored question throughout the history of psychoanalysis, to which L'École lacanienne devoted a colloquium in Paris, 14–15 June 2003.

18 Jacques Lacan, *La logique du fantasme*, 25 January 1967.

19 Jacques Lacan, *L'Acte psychanalytique*, 13 March 1968. On 14 October 1972, Lacan, crossing his t's and dotting his i's, said again very precisely that it was a matter of the passage to the act "not a matter of an acting-out" ("Session at the Belgium School of Psychoanalysis", accessible on *Pas-tout Lacan*, https://ecole-lacanienne.net/bibliolacan/pas-tout).

20 Jacques Lacan, "Resumé du séminaire", *L'Acte psychanalytique*, 1967–1968.

21 Jacques Lacan, *L'Acte psychanalytique*, 24 January 1968.

22 Jacques Lacan, *L'Acte psychanalytique*, 17 January 1968.

23 Jacques Lacan, "Résumé du séminaire", *L'Acte psychanalytique*, 1967–1968.

24 Sigmund Freud, "L'analyse avec fin et l'analyse sans fin" (1937), in *Résultats, idées, problems*, Vol. II (Paris, PUF, 1985, p. 234).

25 Jacques Lacan, *L'Acte psychanalytique*, 13 March 1968.

26 Jacques Lacan, *L'Acte psychanalytique*, 20 March 1968.

27 A demand that Lacan be present at each of the juries of agreement that met to decide whether or not to name Analyst of the School, those in (*The pass*) who

were presented and spoken by (*les passeurs*). Lacan was in an anomalous position, according to a rumour that the other members of the jury turned to him to ask him what he thought of what had been said. And I may be refuted in now stating that no one in the School ever indicated to him that this was not *necessarily* his place.

28 José Attal observed quite rightly that it was not a matter of a failure "of the pass" (*La Passe à plus d'un titre. La troisième propositioned de Jacques Lacan* (Paris, L'Unebévue éditeur, 2012)). Another component of this "failure" was that the Analysts of the School who were invited to judge did not have the least idea what it was all about.

29 Speech during the Congress of *L'École freudiennne* de Paris held in La Grande Motte (published in *Lettres de l'École freudiennne*, no. 15, 1975, accessible through *Pas-tout Lacan*, https://ecole-lacanienne.net/bibliolacan/pas-tout).

30 Would he thus be similar to the Chinese sage? See François Julien, *Un sage est sans idée. Ou l'autre de la philosophy* (Paris, Éditions du Seuil, 2013).

Index

Note: page numbers referring to figures are presented in italics.

Abraham (*Abou Raham*) (father of the multitude // father of nations) 23
Abram (*Abou Ram*) (most high father) 23
act: absence 30; enlightened passage 37; modalities 31; passage. *see* passage to the act. ; preparatory gestures 21
acting, agonistic way (adoption) 3–4
acting-out 35, 74–75; establishment 78; occurrence 75
"acting out" (Lacan) 14; displacement, irruptive intervention 51; irruptive intervention 51
action, violence (perception) 35
acto fallido 7
act, repression 13
Aeneid, The 3
agent of Cahors, lies 53
agieren 74; difference 14
"Air de Sauvages" (talents, display) 1
"*alienating vel*" 30
alienating *vel*, handling (absence) 51
alienation (vector) 77
alienation, *vel* 31
"*Allah Akbar*" 21
Allouch, Jean 8
Al-Mourbitoune 21–22
alterity, Lacan emphasis 5
Althusser, Louis 2, 27–31; act, absence 35; agent, role 28–29; death 32; effect, formulation 32; murderer 8; passage to the act, analysis 74; possession 38; "support," term (explanation) 36
Amante anglaise (name) 64–65
amante/lover 64
American fundamentalism 22
American Pastoral (Roth) 23
"anaclitic relation" 12

analysand: escape 15; impact 29–30; offering 5; remembrance, absence 13; subjective destitution 75; task, qualification 50
analysis: cessation 75–80; setting, defining 17
"analyst-analysand couple" 17
analytical situation, understanding 71
analytic protocol, deviation 16–17
analytics, interplay 37
anatomist, auto-betrayal 7
anglaise (English) 65
Angot, Michel 12
anonymity 32; absence 33
Antigone 22
Antipodes, war (adoption) 3–4
Anzieu, Marguerite 14, 74, 76; Lacan Aimée 52
aporia 37–38
appearing, agonistic way (adoption) 3–4
Aron, Raymond 19
Association freudienne internationale (AFI) transcription 50
ato falho 7
Atta, Mohammed (documents, FBI discovery) *20*, 20–21
audience perplexity, depths 11–12
auditorium, emptiness 27
Aveux de la chair (Foucault) 38
Aztecs, Bousquet body (correspondence) 64

Balmès, François 49
Barbut, Marc 48
Barthes, Roland 33
Beckett, Samuel 33
"being two," tyranny 38
Benslama, Fethi 3–4, 17, 19, 74; clinical discovery 23

ben Talib, Ali 21
between-the-two 51
between-two-deaths 18; space 21, 33
blanchote stone 31
Blanchot, Maurice 31
"blindness," argument 19–20
blindness, impact 19
body, care/blessing 21
Boehringer, Sandra 12
Borromean knot 47
Borromean nature 65
boundaries 17
Bousquet, Marie-Thérèse: animal, resemblance 61; body, correspondence 64; corpse, dispersal 43; corpse, meat in sauce (relationship) 62; deaf-mute condition 54, 60; death 56; head, disappearance 51–52; head, disposal 57; head, Lannes comments 52; housekeeper, role 59; murder 8, 47
Bystander: curses, escape 28–29; escape, method 29

Cabezudo, Iris 35, 74
cachexia, impact 32
Cahors, agent (lies) 53
Calame, Claude 12
Canguilhem, Georges 29
Cartesian subject 30
Caruge, Igor 1
castration 50, 58; "no sexual relation," equivalence 78; pleasure 77; post-castration passage to the act 79
catastrophic fact 71
Catholicism, Althusser reconnection 38
childhood memory, recounting 28
choice: criterion 74; heuristic nature 50
Chrysippus, human corpse digestion 64
claim (affirmation) 15
clinical order, criterion 74
cogito, impact 50
Cogitore, Clément 1
cogito, unfolding 31
"Come!," word (speaking) 36, 38
community, "fundamentalist" nature (acknowledgement) 22
condemnation (act, passage) 14–18
condemnation (affirmation) 15
confinements, agent role 28–29
"confinements," discussion 28–29
conscious thought, activity (absence) 37
"constructions" (Freud) 37

contract, usefulness 17
Coste, Marina 28
counter-transference, classical theories 71
countertransference, seizing 71–72
"couple," term (impact) 38
creative ignorance 6
Csonka, Margarethe (laughter/scorn) 13
Cynics, necrophagia 64

dance, sporting performance (comparison) 1
dans un premier temps 27
"*déchariter*" 15
Decorpeliada, Marco 5
defilement, focus 22
de la Trinité, Marie 76
de Libera, Alain 28–29
Dembele, Bintou 1
Depardon, Raymond 2
"de-radicalisation" 23
Descartes, René 30
Descola, Philippe 12
dèsêtre (un-being) 58–59, 75, 77
"destiny of having no place" 34
"destructivity" 12
Detienne, Marcel 12
de Urtebey, Louise 70–74
Deutung 8
diagonals, involvement 49
Diet, Thomas 1
"disappeared," word (implication) 37
distributive criterion, presence 3
divine law, relinquishment 22–23
divine will, phrases (recalling) 21
Djihadisme (Rogozinski) 19
"does the job" (*fair affaire*) 2
Donnadieu, Marguerite 57
"do the trick" (*fait l'affaire*), avoidance 2
dream: constitution 5; content 18; occurrence 4
Droit, Roger-Pol 19
drowning (act, passage) 14–18
drown the fish (*noyed le poisson*) 15
Du gout de l'autre. Fragments d'un discours cannibale (Kilani) 64
Duras, Marguerite 2, 33, 42; game, playing 45; style, attack 53

Écrits (Lacan) 38
effet-d'entre 46
égout (sewer), Lannes transformation 65
Einfall (thought) 55

"Either I do not think, or I am not" (Lacan) 47–51; Schéma 1 *48*; Schéma 2 *48*; Schéma 3 *49*, 77; Schéma 4 *50*; Schéma 5 *58*; Schéma 6 *59*; Schéma 7 *62*
el-Assad, Bashar 23
Elsaesser, Thomas 7
enemy, misnaming 19
en glaise (glazed/in clay) 64
enlightened passage to the act 70, 78–79
"enlightened passage to the act" (Lacan meaning) 37
En prison, les paroles de djihadistes (Monod) 22
entre (between) 47; reboundings 46
entre-deux 18
epic leap: clinical discovery 35; completion, absence 62; consideration 3–4, 74; co-presence 8; discrimination 4; incompleteness 57–59; inscription 58; irreducibility, assertion 51; jihadist act, contrast 17–18; occurrence 22–23, 75; passage to the act (contrast) 46–48; passage to the act (relationship) 42; presence 38; thinking leap, equivalence 51; traits 56
"epic leap" (Benslama) 3; gesture 4
"epic leap," naming (question) 35
"episode," observation 76
equivocation, resonance 52
erotic foreplay 36
erotic responses, problems 71
escape, possibility (absence) 47–48
Essais (Montaigne) 64
European intellectuals, perception 12
event: absence 15; defining 19; generic term, consideration 2–3; significance 8
evil 12–13; counteraction, good (impact) 13
existential trajectory (break/bifurcation) 3–4
ex-nihilo, Duras invention (absence) 43–44
explanation, absence 43

"facet of the act," emphasis 7
Falwell, Jerry 22
fantasm, path 75
farewell letter, *normalien* writing 29
Fehlleistung (failed act), contradictoriness 7
Ferenczi, Sándor (practice) 17
finance of mind (*finance d'estrit*) 7

fineness of mind (*finesse d'esprit*) 7
Finkiel, Emmanuel 54
fluidity, speed (relationship) 1
Foucault, Michel 3, 6, 29, 31, 38
fragmentation (act, passage) 14–18
fragmentation, study 6
free association 77
Frege, Gottlob 30
French (language), mistreatment/ deformation 47
Freudian ternary 1
Freud, Sigmund 33–34, 71; discourse, contrast 12; dream/culpability 34; practice 17; *Psychopathology of Everyday Life* 7; rules, revolt 73; *Talmud*, distancing 8; Vienna ostracisation/London arrival 6

Gide, André 13, 29
Gilgamesh 3
Gitaï, Amos 18
God: absence 21, 53; expectation 38; Lannes, reconnection 52; love (story) 56; presentation 3–4; questioning 22; substitute 56; unconscious, equivalence 8
gods, inspiration/possession 67
Graham, Billy 22
"guardian of the setting" role 16–17

Halevy, Efraim 20
hallucinated presence, destruction 36
Harry Potter (saga) 23
hate-filled impulse, repression 13
hatred: emergence 12; jouissance, presence 12
"health professionals," society demands 16–17
"*Hegel et Freud. Essai d'une confrontation interpretative*" (Kojève) 30–31
Hinduism 28
historicised meaning, criterion 4
history: recourse 4; rejection (Lacan) 8
Hocquenghem, Guy 38
holy war (jihad), waging 19
"Homeric anger" 46
"*Hommage fait à Marguerite Duras du Ravissement de Lol V. Stein*" (Lacan) 42–43
"honest man" 12
human corpses, eating 64
Hussein, Imam 3–4

Index

ideality 18
"I do not think" 63; choice 77
ignorance, passion 6
immortality 28
"impaired judgement," presentation 11
impious, massacre 4
Indes galantes (Rameau) 1
In God We Trust motto, adoption 22
inhibition: consequences 5; envisage, absence 5
"initiatory" journey, description 23
interlocutor, defeat (admission) 65
International Psychoanalytical Association (IPA) 70–75
interpellation 27
interpretation, production 51
Intolérable dureté du durer (intolerable hardness of lasting) 28
"introjection" 12
involuntary psychiatric hospitalisation 2
"Irma's injection" (dream) 16
irruptive interventions 50–51
ISIS, theological thinking 22, 23
Islam, commitment 21–22
Israel events, Hamas understanding 20
Israeli-Palestine conflict 18
it/her, burial 52
"it-is-said" ("*on-dit*") 33, 34

Jainism, approach 23
"*je t'entre*" ("I between/enter you") 47
jihad (holy war): *j-h-d* root, meaning 19; waging 19
jihadism, stakes 22–23
jihadist act, epic leap (contrast) 17–18
jihadists: humanity, re-giving 23; "pass to the act" 4; signed text trace (9/11) 3; spirituality degree 20; terrorists, comparison 19
jihadist war, seeking 21
jouissance 12; absence 77, 78; barrier 16–17; desire 23; reworked jouissance, agent responsibility 15

kamikaze, term (usage) 19
Kierkegaard, Søren 28
Kilani, Mondher 64
"Kingdom Racially Uplifted Mighty Praise" (Krump) dancers, invitation 1
Kissinger, Henry 1
Klein group: involutive operations 49; mathematical properties, usage (avoidance) 49; softening/connections 48

knowledge, use 12
Kojève, Alexandre 30–31
Koran, reading 21

labor limae (Horace) 15–16
"Lacanian" drivel, reading 17–18
Lacanian pastoral, evocation 15–16
Lacanian psychoanalysts: manager role 14; "new deal" Lacanian psychoanalyst 15
Lacanian relic 3
Lacanian solution 13
Lacan, Jacques 4, 8. *see also* "Either I do not think, or I am not"; "acting-out" 14; clinical observation 5; diagonals, involvement 49; "enlightened passage to the act" (meaning) 37; history rejection 8; irregularities 50; *La Relation d'objet* seminar 14; practice 17, 29; quadrangular schema 57; responsibility, quota 14; *vel*, term (mentioning) 30–31; "wild transference" 14
L'Acte analytique seminar 15
l'acte manqué 7
l'amante (the lover) 64
L'Amante anglaise (Duras) 2, 8, 31, 42, 44; consideration 51, 64–65; epic leap 45–47; psychoanalyst, link 80; reader, decision 56; reading 75; thread, following 57
la menthe anglaise (English mint) 64–65
Lamy, Robert 45; questioning 53
Lannes, Claire 2, 37; actions, strangeness 54; acts, analysis 55; epic leap 77; God reconnection 52; head 56; information, providing 51–52; initial absence 45; meat, disgust 61–62; murderer 8, 43; passage to the act 61, 74; praying 56; suicide attempt 57; tranquillisation 57
Lannes, Pierre: remark, ignoring 46; testimony 60–61; voice recording 45
lapsus 43
La Relation d'objet seminar (Lacan) 14
L'Arrêt de mort ("The Stopping of Death") (Blanchot) 31
La "Solution" du passage à l'acte 63
La Tentation radicale (Galland/Muxel) 20
L'Avenir dure longtemps ("The future lasts a long time") (Melogno) 27–28, 32–34; manuscript, passage (reading) 35

L'École freudienne 29
L'École lacanienne, Benslama invitation 3
L'École Normale Supérieure 29
Le Détracteur (Anzieu) 52–53
Legend of the Ages, The 3
Le Ravissement de Lol V. Stein (Duras) 42
Les Folies raisonnantes (Sérieux/ Capgras) 54
Les Viaducs de la Seine-et-Oise (Duras) 42, 44, 54
Le Théâtre de l'Amante anglaise (Duras) 42, 44, 53
Lévi-Strauss, Claude 38
Levov, Seymour 23
life history 2–3
lip-reading, usage 60
"living in hell without hell" 23
logos 12
Lord of the Rings, The (saga) 23
love-making 36
love, survival 55

madness, emergent point 2
"magic circle," absence 52
magic circle, joining 42
Mahabharata 3
"man craving fresh brains" case, revisit 74–75
martyrdom: granting 21; jihadist candidate 3–4
Marx, Karl 35
"*Massage à l'acte*" 31
Mathematics, word structure (meaning) 48
Mauss, Marcel 2
meaning: criterion 74; recourse 4
melancholy, moral fault 5
Melogno, Ricardo 27
mental illness, paradigm 3
metonymy 27, 61
Milner, Jean-Claude 28–29, 33
mise en abime 45
moksha 28
momentum, trace 1
Monod, Guillaume 22–23
"Montagne Pavée" viaduct 44, *44*
Montagne Pavée viaduct, examination 55
Montaigne 65
moral considerations, dispensing 70
Morgan, Augustus de 47; laws, representation 48
mourning 51–57; ritual 52; ritual, resolution 56

movement, extension 13
murder (act), trace (absence) 35
mûthos 12

narrative, coherence 5
necrophagia 64
negated ensembles, union 48
negating disquiet 34
negativised *cogito*, dismemberment 48
neologism 47
neutral (Neutral) 16, 33–34; intervention 34; name, replacement 35; point, reaching (absence) 34
niederkommen (*Niederkommen*) 60; equivocation 13
Nietzsche, Friedrich (God) 55
non-achievement, return 63
non-believers 21
non-ending 32
non-existent Other 23
non-place, justness 37
noyed le poisson (drown the fish) 15

object a, topology 76
Odyssey, The 3
Oedipal sexual activity, imagining 73
off-kilter speaking 33
Other (*l'Autresexe*) 46–47, 78; arrival 47; definition, change 47; desire 50; existence 8; non-existent Other 23; positioning 38; relevance 38
Other as place 57
O'Toole, Fintan 8

Palestine, crusaders (approach) 4
Pandora's box, opening 71
"Papin affair" 2
Papin, Christine 32; passage to the act, realisation 63; statement, echo 47
Papin sisters 14, 51; act, passage 31–32; crime 2, 3
parapraxis: acting 35; constitution 5; failed act 7; occurrence 4
parlêtres (speaking-beings) 47
"passage," suggestion 13
passage to the act 31–32; abandonment, criteria 74; acknowledgement 37; actions 35; actuality 11; another place, naming 78–79; characteristic 37; difference 31; drowning/ fragmentation/condemnation 14–18; enlightened passage to the act 70, 78–79; envisaging 16, 70; epic leap, contrast 46–48; epic leap, relationship

42; evacuation 15; explanation, perversity (relationship) 22; facing 32; impact 12; incompleteness 59–63; invocation 36; irreducibility, assertion 51; Lacanian conception 13; logic clarity, providing (inability) 12; meaning, determination 37; occurrence 75; presentation 51; religious/practical instructions, collection 20–21; strangeness 9
"passage to the act" 4
"Passer à l'acte" dossier 73–74
patients: attacks, analyst survival 72; hatred, emergence 12
Paul of Tarsus (Damascus approach) 3–4
people, jargonisation (question) 12
perturbado 7
petit a: inscription 50, 58; location 63; object 63, 64; subject, connection 62
phallus, absence 47
pharmakon 65
"phobia" 21
physical death 28
plates, breaking 60–61
Plotinus, support 23
poétereau (unremarkable poet) 53
poetry, thinking (impact) 32
point of departure, passing/returning 78
poisoner of Chambéry 11
poisoner's personality 11
Porte d'Orléans, Lannes arrival 57
post mortem publication 34
power, conquest 1
"power of things" 35
practising, prevention 17
pre-meditation, absence 37
"Proposition d'octobre 1967 sur la psychanalyste de l'école" 79–80
psychiatric discourse/practices, objects 1–2
psychiatric knowledge, trap (avoidance) 22
psychiatric/psychoanalytical practice/theory, aegis 2
psychoanalysis: effects 29; origin 33–34; plural form 70; questions 6; setting, rules 72; termination, impossibility 71; undergoing 5
psychoanalysts. *see* Lacanian psychoanalysts: "guardian of the setting" role 16–17; second patient, status 72
psychoanalysts, passage to the act 73; problem 71; viewpoint 72

psychology, radical rejection (nonacknowledgement) 29
Psychopathology of Everyday Life (Freud) 7
psychopathology, rewriting 5
psychotherapy, qualification 64
psy function 5
pulsion, path 75
"pure love" (qualification) 56
pure supposed 29
purity, focus 22

Rabilloux, Amélie: murder 47; trial 43–44
Rachiki, Brahim 1
radicalised, racist connotations 19–20
radical silence 33
Ragond, Marcel 54
Rank, Otto 3
ratonnade ("racist attack" translation) 20
reaction, impact 7
registers 70; change 14; disparity 14; distinction 30
reincarnation 28
"Remembering, repeating and working-through" (Freud) 13, 73
re-settings 63–64; pivot 64
"resistants" (Vichy name) 19
revealed-Being 30–31
revealing-Being 30–31
Rêver compte ("To dream matters") 29
reworked jouissance, agent responsibility 15
Ricœur, Paul 8
Rignieri, Alfonso 45
River Oise, tributary 55
River Seine, Lannes visit 57
Rogozinski, Jacob 19
Roy, Claude 42
rumour, feeding 33
Rytman, Hélène: hallucinated presence 37–38; murder 8, 30, 34–36

"saga," term (appearance) 23
Sageman, Marc 19
Said, Edward 12, 19
"Saint-Benoît group" 42
Saint Just 22
Saint-Simon, Henri de 35
s'Autreposer 47
Savigny-sur-Orge, train travel 54, 55
School of Criminology (University of Montreal) (Foucault invitation) 6

second death 28; reference 31
"seizing" (*sésir*) 37
Sekel, Henri 11
"self-betrayal by lapsus" 7
self-revelation, practise 71
separation, movement 3–4
September 11 2001 20–23; documents, FBI discovery *20*, 20–21; God, questioning 22; jihadists, impact 43
sésir/désir, relationship 36
sésir, hallucination (absence) 36
sex, second analytic 37
sexual act: "Come!," word (speaking) 36; passage, condemnation 16; psychoanalyst passage 72–73
sexual couplet, Other 46–47
sexual relation: inexistence 17; non-existence, affirmation 47; scent 71; "seizing" (*sésir*) 37
sexual relation, existence 8; attempt/illusion 38; belief 17
sexual union, *jouissance* (absence) 78
Shakespeare is hard, but so if life (O'Toole) 8
shiny tomorrows, promise 15
"short" session 17
signed text, trace 3
signified, fascination 8
Si l'analyste passe à l'acte ("If the analyst passes to the act") (de Urtebey) 70, 73
Silesiuis, Angelus 23
"slow work of the lime" (*labor limae*) (Horace) 15–16
social domain, madness/psychiatry (emergent point) 2
social law, specification 16–17
Société nationale de Chemins de fer (SNCF) (French National Railway Company) agent 53–54, 55; lie 56
space (*entre-deux*) 18
speaking, agonistic way (adoption) 3–4
speed, fluidity (relationship) 1
spiritual crusade, Christianity engagement 22
spirituality 18; exclusion 19
"split" personality, presentation 11
sporting performance, dance (comparison) 1
Star Wars (saga) 23
Steiner, George 23
Stoics, necrophagia 64
structure, negativities 78

subject history, assumption 4
subjective destitution 75
"subjective destitution" 15; banner 77
subject, jump 58
subject, second death (depriving) 33
"support": double presence 37; meaning, Althusser clarification 36
suspension of judgement (*épokhē*) 43
"symbolic act" 13, 14
symbolic enunciation 31
Symbolic, Imaginary, Real (S.I.R. registers) 70
symptom: constitution 5; occurrence 4
symptomatic act, acting 35
Szabo, Denis 6

Talmud, Freud distancing 8
"technique," indications 17
terrorism: act 19; consideration 21; religious dimension perception (prevention), blindness (impact) 19
terrorists: "radicalism," explanation 19–20; West (people), contrast 22
terrorist, term (Western use) 19
terror, spreading 18–19
tetrahedron apices, subject (jump/reach) 58, 63
"The badly named passage to the act" (*Le mal nommé passage à l'acte*) 12–13
Théolleyre, Jean-Marc 44, 47
theological thinking (ISIS) 22, 23
thinking: dispensing 76; impossibility 31–32
thinking leap, epic leap (equivalence) 51
Thomas l'Obscur, mentioning (Lacan seminar) 31
thought: colonialism, cessation 12; imperialism 37; realisation 31
"tombstone of silence" 34
"total social fact" concept (Mauss) 2
Tower, Lucy 71
trace, effacement 7, 35
transference: analysand enactment 29–30; establishment 78; invitation 5; love, true love (equivalence, denial) 72; mirror 71; position, interrogation 17; vector 77
transferential shift 30
"transgression" (word), awaiting 16
transgression, term (usage) 72
transgressive sexual act, passage 17, 73
"trauma" (word), awaiting 16–17

truth, vector 77
Tudal, Antoine 46
Twelve Days (Depardon) 2
Twin Towers, destruction 12

"unanalysed" aspect 78
un-being. *see dèsêtre*
"un-being" ("*dèsêtre*") 15
unconscious: formations 6; Lacan definition 4
unexpressed disapproval, act 7
University of Amsterdam 7
University of Montreal, School of Criminology (Foucault invitation) 6
"uprising": irruptive intervention 50; term, usage 31

vel, term (mentioning) 30–31
venom ("poison"), perception 15
verbal exchanges, avoidance 51–52

Vinatier Psychiatric Hospital (Lyon), cases 2
violation, term (usage) 72
Viorne (town), murder location 54

Wagner, Ernst 35, 74
West of the Jordan River (Gitaï) (documentary) 18
why (question), answering (incapability) 11
"wild transference" (Lacan) 14
Winkler, John 12
Wittgenstein, Ludwig 14
word structure, meaning 48

"young homosexual woman" (*Niederkommen*) 60

Zenon, human corpse digestion 64
Zidane, Zinédine 6

For Product Safety Concerns and Information please contact our EU representative GPSR@taylorandfrancis.com
Taylor & Francis Verlag GmbH, Kaufingerstraße 24, 80331 München, Germany

www.ingramcontent.com/pod-product-compliance
Lightning Source LLC
Chambersburg PA
CBHW050542300426
44113CB00012B/2226